SUNSHINE AND SHADOW

The story of Wilfred Crone's life spans most of the twentieth
century, starting in poverty and struggle in North East
England, emigrating to farmlands in Australia where he
learnt to love and respect the animals, and returning to
Britain where he finally discovered a harmonious
and joyful way of life.

Wilfred Crone.

SUNSHINE
and
SHADOW

An Autobiography

Wilfred Crone

Illustrations by Anna Shiels

Harry Mather

First published 1998 by Harry Mather, 6 Hayes Avenue,
Bournemouth BH7 7AD, England

ISBN 0 9531985 0 2

Printed and bound in England by J. W. Arrowsmith Ltd.,
Winterstoke Road, Bristol

CONTENTS

ACKNOWLEDGEMENTS

The photograph on the frontispiece is by Ernest Woolford, and that on page 143 by Monica Harvey.

A CHILDHOOD IN TYNESIDE

NEARLY FORTY YEARS AGO, a lady converted me to vegetarianism, and since then I have progressed dietetically, until I now live mainly on fruit. Moving from ghastly flesh-eating, to lacto-vegetarian, to vegan, to fruitarian — and my only regret is that I wasn't a fruitarian from birth. You may well wonder what made me so dedicated — to answer that I must tell you something of my early environment.

I was brought up during the early days of the century in the industrial North, when families were large, and fighting and heavy drinking were the hallmarks of a 'real man'. Children were to be seen but not heard, and preferably not even seen.

I remember one Sunday morning when there was snow on the ground being sent to the local shop with a jug for a gill of milk. Polly Beck, who was eight years old and in my class at school, came running in after me. Her feet were bare and steam was rising from under her long, thin, torn mac.

Mrs Wilson served her with a packet of gravy salt and asked why she was steaming so much.

'Have you run all the way?'

'Yes,' she replied, 'I've just got out of the tub to get me mother the gravy salt.' Up North, a tub was used for the dual purpose of possing the clothes and at weekends as a bath, placed in front of the fire. I remember Mrs Wilson saying to a woman in the shop after she'd gone, 'That child was naked under that coat and was soaking wet.'

I missed her at school and so after about a fortnight I asked a boy from the Pit Square, close to Polly's home, what had happened.

'Polly Beck? — she's deed.' He answered in our Geordie dialect. Evidently, there were no awkward questions asked, no enquiry, just one less mouth to feed. In those days many of our parents, teachers and adults in general seemed to regard us children as just unavoidable nuisances.

Starting school

I started school, a catholic convent, at the age of four. My elder brother

Jim took me in a pushchair. He ran all the way down the 'private road' with the pram tipped back because the two front wheels were missing, dumped me near the tall iron gates that led into the convent drive, and then dashed off to his council school. I stood wondering what was going to happen next. A smell of carbolic soap hovered around the area and my future classmates played in an apprehensive way. Eventually, two or three nuns appeared. One blew a whistle and immediately all the chatter and milling around ceased. Another whistle and there was a scatter and shuffling into a semblance of two lines. A nun came over and asked me if I'd come to start school.

'Yes,' I answered.

'How old are you?'

'Four.'

'Well, go back home and tell your mother that you can't start until you are five.'

When I got home, my mother rose to the occasion.

'Go back again tomorrow and tell her that you *are* five.'

The ruse must have worked, because I remember one of the nuns had to carry me while the rest marched down the long drive to the school, kept in some sort of step by a nun clicking a wooden clapper like a big clothes peg, ' left – left – left'.

My next recollection of the convent school, and a painful one at that, was of a five year old girl called Madgy Dag — a child with the face of an angel but the heart of a devil. She used to fall into line behind me and while we were shuffling along to the click, click, click of the nun's pacer, I would suddenly let out a mighty yell and barge forward, sending the kids in front scattering. Madgy Dag had rammed a pin into my backside. Time and time again I was caned for sending the kids sprawling, but I never split on her. Whether it was from a sense of misplaced loyalty or fear of more severe retribution I cannot remember, but I was terrified. In my desperation I grew cunning and used to hide behind the wall while the others lined up and then run to join the line well behind my tormentress. However, she countered this by simply side-stepping and shuffling into the line again as I passed. Once or twice, I remember, the nun asked her if she'd done anything to me. 'No, Sister Hopper,' she always replied, with eyes cast down in deep humility, 'I didn't touch him.' Madgy Dag, as I said before, was a devil incarnate with the face of an angel, but if ever there's a post mortem on me, I'm sure they'll find her name tattooed with pin pricks on my nether regions.

Sister Hopper taught us the catechism and gave us lessons on religion. Sometimes the class had to answer questions in turn. Once I was asked:

'If you were in a dark room under the ground with no doors or windows, would God be able to see you?'

'No,' I replied with conviction, 'no one could see me.'

'Sit down,' she said tartly, 'Next!'

'Yes,' said the budding saint next to me, 'God could see me.'

'And why,' she asked the class, 'could God see you?'

'Because,' they all chorused, 'God can see you everywhere.'

How was I to know at that age that God was greater than Houdini?

Our house and the farm

From the long drive leading to the convent (called 'the private road') I could see our back door. It was at the top of the concrete steps leading from the back yard we shared with the butcher's shop below us and I remember the dislike I used to have for my own home. Our father was never cruel to us. We were just ignored. He died of cancer. He suffered agonies for three years and all through the nights we could hear him at intervals moaning with pain. The memory of his suffering made such an impression on me that it gave me a strong impulse in later years to seek healthy ways of living that would avoid such an agonising end.

On one side of the private road leading to the convent was a high wooden fence, and on the other side a hawthorn hedge bordering the 'buttercup and daisy field'. Only the most daring amongst us ever dared to crawl through. To us it was enchanted territory, to be seen but not stepped upon. A story was whispered around that a boy had once been caught and never seen again.

I remember one Saturday morning climbing up the wall bordering the main road and looking into the field and seeing, to my horror, that two friends of mine had been caught by the farmer. They were Walter and Betty Hunt, an inseparable pair. The boy was about eight years old and the girl about six. The farmer held the boy's outstretched arm and the sister held his other hand, pulling the opposite way. They presented a slow moving tableau to my goggle-eyed fascination; for to be caught by the farmer, or by Sticky the policeman, was the dual fear of every kid in the neighbourhood. Slowly he pulled the boy towards the farmhouse, with his sister hanging on, trying to pull the other way. It says a lot for the girl's courage, because she wouldn't let go and yet they must both have been terrified of the unknown but terrible punishment awaiting them when the farmhouse was reached. After what seemed an eternity of dread to me and no doubt to them as well, the farmer suddenly clouted Walter Hunt across the ear with his free hand and let them go. I've never seen kids run so fast. Within seconds they covered about a hundred yards of the hallowed buttercup and daisy field and were through the hawthorn hedge onto the private road.

Now I don't doubt that the farmer had to make sure hordes of children didn't invade his pasture land, but why such drawn out fear for the odd few who ventured in? Surely he must have known the temptation a grass field held for us. The road that passed our house separated congested streets of Victorian houses from farmland that stretched beyond the convent. We lived at the top of the street and from the attic windows we had a really beautiful view, with the farmhouse buildings on the right.

Beneath our home was a butcher's shop, whilst the shop next to that was often empty. Various people tried to make a go of it but usually left after a few months. In the third shop a cobbler plied his trade. He, with his wife and Violet his daughter, lived above the premises next to us. When the noise from our house became unbearable, they used to thump on the dividing wall. The farmhouse was nearly opposite and I was sometimes sent there with a tin can and a halfpenny for a gill of milk, but I was always apprehensive when I entered the farmyard for it was enemy territory for me and I felt vulnerable to being caught.

A narrow escape

I remember once when they were haymaking, my sister and I with four or five of her girl friends ventured across to a far field where they were building ricks. We moved slowly across the first field, ready to run for our lives at any sign of being seen. The farm buildings were about a hundred yards to our left and we kept wary eyes on them in case anyone came out. The men were at the far side of the second field and seemed too busy to notice us and we were partly screened by a dividing hedge.

Eventually we reached the hayfield and with great trepidation crept cautiously through gaps in the hedge — and lo! we stood on hallowed ground. It was even more hallowed and sacred than the field we had crossed! The stubble under our feet and the sweet smell of the hay gave us the feeling of a mysterious, fascinating and beautifully scented world. Now we stood like startled deer, surprised at our daring. Small, round, pointed hayricks were dotted around the field awaiting collection. One was about twenty yards off. Dare we venture so far? Our feelings of standing in paradise were tempered with real fear for we were a long way from the road. Anyone could run from the farmhouse and cut off our retreat and an uninterrupted chase by adults would probably end in our capture.

Suddenly there was a shout. The farmer had seen us. We stood for a moment rooted to the spot. He shouted to a couple of hands and pointed in our direction. They started running towards us and as they took chase, we took wings. After scrambling through the hedge, the girls, to my dismay, ran obliquely across the field towards the road, and although it led nearer to our homes it was a longer way to run — and we would pass the field entrance to the farm on the danger side, and with a stone wall to climb over at the end. I remember running over the hard, pitted ground where the cows milled around at milking time, but I never faltered for I think my guardian angel held me by the scruff of the neck, helping me along. Luckily no one came out of the farmhouse to cut off our retreat. When we reached the stone wall opposite our house, I remembered, from previous short excursions into the field, where one or two jutting stones gave a foothold. I was over the wall in no time. The girls also scrambled over and we all landed on the pavement more or less together.

As we panted for breath, we took stock of our surroundings and possible casualties, but there were none. Suddenly, one of the girls noticed little, pot-bellied me standing in their midst.

'Bessie, your brother's here!' Their startled eyes of fear gave way to wider eyes of astonishment. One or two put their arms around me. I was a hero!

'How did you run so fast?'

'How did you climb the wall?'

'How did you run as fast as us?'

'How were you not caught?'

I looked at them, drinking in the adulation and lapping up the praise, but even at that age I knew that if I hadn't run so fast, they would have left me to my fate. In that immediate past we had experienced the risk of life or death. The law of the survival of the fittest had motivated each one of us to run like hell, without heed for the others, be it a big girl or little me.

A sensitive soul

It was about this time that Dolly Kircup loomed large in my life. Everyone at school knew that she was 'upper class' because she had two inches of lace showing on her bloomers below her dress. Girls at our school probably thought they were lucky to have bloomers, never mind lace on the bottom. Not that I had any particular regard for Dolly herself, but I used to be invited by her auntie, with whom she lived, to play with her niece in their backyard. This meant a free tea, which to me was the highlight of the afternoon. At about four o'clock auntie would appear at the top of the long flight of steps leading to the brick-walled yard. They, by the way, lived above Lumley's barber shop and Mrs Wilson's grocery store. She would come down carrying a tray of thinly cut bread and butter and two glasses of lemonade. The bread was always both brown and white, cut in quarter slices, with the pile on my plate higher than Dolly's. 'Now, Dolly,' auntie would say, as she laid the tray on a low wickerwork table, 'try to eat it all. If you can't, try to eat as much as you can.' We used to sit on three-legged stools and while Dolly consumed one or two quarters at a snail's pace, my pile would disappear like dew on the mountain when the sun rises; and when my plate was barren of any more sustenance, Dolly would invariably say, 'Help me with some of mine.' I would immediately start demolition work on her bread, but I always left some. Whether it was from diplomacy or satiation, I cannot remember. Later on, auntie would appear again to take the tray away and express great delight that Dolly had eaten so much. If only she'd taken a look at my stomach, she might have guessed where all the bread and butter had gone.

Sometimes, probably on birthdays, her backyard would be filled with girls for the afternoon and it was at these times that I used to feel a social outcast. Auntie would come down the steps with various games for us to play: Ludo, tiddlewinks, snakes and ladders and so on. Before she left auntie would say, 'If any of the girls want to use the lavatory,' (which was in the backyard next to the coalhouse) 'they can use ours, but if Wilfred wants to go, he has to go home and use his own.' This used to puzzle me. Why always me? Why couldn't Violet Sommers or Sally Jordan or someone else use theirs for a change? Why always me? In the end I thought I must be a social outcast for some obscure reason. Even our Bessie could use their lavatory, but not me.

Dolly was shy and if a stranger spoke to her, she would cover her eyes with her arm and just wait for them to go away, but even as a child she was very sweet natured and graceful. Later in life, she became a good ballet dancer. Another point in her favour of which I was always aware, was that her backyard was always cleaner than ours.

Kite flying

We shared our backyard with Mr Hardy, the butcher in the shop downstairs, and a better natured man it would be hard to find. He always gave us good weight and wasn't averse to sending upstairs a free lump of meat now and again, yet he couldn't have made much money himself — not in our district. Around his shop was a high rail with rollers attached to huge hooks for hanging the carcasses. If I became too much of a nuisance running in and out of the shop, he used to exact penance by hoisting me up and

hanging me by the pants on one of the hooks. Mr Hardy and the customers thought this most amusing, but I didn't. Suspended about eight feet above the sawdusted floor and having a bird's eye view of the customers being served with their 'half a pound of drippin' and a pound of stewin' steak' wasn't my idea of a good joke. He never left me there for long though. After a while he would take me down and the 'nuisance' wouldn't trouble him again — at least not for a day or two.

Kites were all the rage at that time; not the flash affairs one buys in shops, but homemade ones. We would split canes and tie them with thread at the cross section into the shape of a cross, then stick newspaper over them and attach a tail of string with cross scallops of folded paper at intervals to keep the tail down and the head up. Usually, with our aeronautics being a bit awry, the kite would rise at an alarming angle as we ran down the lane to give it buoyancy, then suddenly it would change its mind and dive to the ground at an equally alarming angle, bent on its own destruction. The result would be a sorry mess of torn paper and broken canes.

Sometimes Mr Hardy would laboriously make me a kite while the shop was quiet, then send me down the back lane to try it out. I would return, out of breath.

'It won't go up, Mr Hardy.'

'Right, give it to me, laddie.' I'd pass it over the gory chopping block.

'We'll shorten the tail.' He'd swipe a length off with the meat chopper.

'Now see if that works.' I would try it out down the lane, only to return again.

'It's going side to side but not in the air, Mr Hardy.'

He would take his round straw hat off and hold it just above his head, ready to put it on again as soon as a brainwave came. Back would go the straw hat.

'Right, we'll try a bigger paper at the end of the tail.'

So it would go on. I think that, big as he was, his aeronautics were about as hazy as mine. Eventually, probably out of desperation, he made a new kite out of greaseproof paper and came with me to help get it airborne. It was a gusty, windy day. I ran down the lane holding the string and when the string tightened, Mr Hardy gave the kite a swoop into the air. It sailed majestically up and up! I was overjoyed. I didn't even have to run. It swayed and dived, then climbed again and the string, pulling and relaxing in my hand, made it feel like something alive. I was fascinated and also bewildered that it was at last really working.

The butcher came running down the lane. I think the fact that it was majestically soaring in the air high above the houses was as big a surprise to him as it was to me. 'Let out some more string, laddie,' he called. 'Give it a pull — go back a bit — now forward a bit.' To show me how to do it, he took the string and became engrossed in the pastime himself. I couldn't blame him for it was a kite of his own making, swooping and soaring like a bird enjoying celestial freedom. Suddenly I became aware of two or three women calling from the top of the lane.

'Mr Hardy, there's no one in the shop!'

'Mr Hardy, have you got any rabbits in?'

'Mr Hardy, can I get served?'

He took a last lingering look at the kite, then handed the string back to me. 'Here, keep tight hold. Keep it till I come back.' We had a right royal time that day!

Some people wondered how he'd missed being conscripted into the army. He was certainly a big, fit-looking man and every second poster on the walls, vans or hoardings was of a moustached soldier pointing his finger directly at you, with the caption 'Kitchener Wants You!' He may have had an infirmity, or perhaps butchering was considered an occupation necessary for the public welfare. I don't know the answer but, as far as I was concerned, he was far better employed making me kites that flew than defending the realm.

Trouser trouble

'Wilfred Crone,' said Sister Hopper, 'go to the back of the class and fasten your trouser buttons up.' We were playing ring-a-ring-a-roses and singing the chorus as we ran around with hands joined. When the 'all fall down' part came, everyone sat on the floor and I unwittingly became a five-year-old flasher. Then we got up and started again. I went to the back of the classroom, lifted up my hole ridden 'gansey' and studied the safety pins fastening my trousers to my shirt. Everything seemed in order to me. My failing, I was made to realise later, was a fat stomach, because anything below the waistline I couldn't see — a case of out of sight, out of mind. (The fat stomach, by the way, was more likely to be caused by malnutrition than over-eating, because during World War I grey bread with a thin spreading of margarine and a few near-black potatoes was often considered a meal.) Back to the circle I went.

'Wilfred Crone,' I was told in a sharper voice at the next 'all fall down', 'go to the back of the class and do your trousers up!' This had me stumped. Here was I having a whale of a time, yet constantly having to leave the revelry for no apparent reason. At the back of the room again, I tried to solve the offending mystery. Safety pins all right, shirt tucked in — so back to the circle I went, but rather diffidently this time, and joined in the ring-a-ring-a-roses. The game was becoming a nightmare. This time, at the 'all fall down' the nun came around with an air of finality, took me by the hand and led me unceremoniously to the back of the empty desks, bent down and tapped the member that's only sported by the male of the species with her finger and said, 'Put that thing away.' She then ran back to the other children as if all the demons of hell were chasing her!

Nevertheless, I was always conscious of bias at the convent. I don't know whether it was because our family wasn't Catholic, or it may have been my scruffy appearance — for my mother never got any of us ready for school. She never got up before nine o'clock in the morning and I never knew that beds were meant to be made until later in life. We just got into them the way we'd got out. Three of us slept in one bed and four in the other. Often I'd waken in the morning with one foot on a different side of the sheet than the other, having gone through a hole in the sheet during the night.

School lessons

At the convent there was a row of small blackboards stuck on the wall along one side of the classroom. 'Now,' Sister Hopper would call, 'at the word 'go', I want you all to run to a blackboard, ready for the next lesson.' We used chalk for drawing on them. Sometimes we had to draw an animal. If a house had to be drawn, we usually drew a table and chairs in the living room and a bed in the bedroom. I can still remember how at one lesson we drew a walking stick, then another with the handle touching the first. 'Now that is an "n",' we were told. 'Now draw another with the handle touching the second walking stick. Now that is an "m".' However, there were not enough boards for everyone in the class and a few on the far side of the class, having further to run, were seldom lucky. More often than not, I seemed to be one of the unlucky ragamuffins.

Another event that distressed me once was taking cakes to a school party, then having to sit and watch while the other children ate them. Funnily, I remember feeling more sorry for my mother than for myself, because she'd paid tuppence for them. Every Friday morning we were all asked to bring something to school to eat after dinner. All the offerings were pooled and a party was held in the front of the classroom. Anyone who hadn't brought anything had to sit at their desk and wait for the party to finish. A few of us never even expected to join in. We just waited with childlike resignation for the 'Rothschilds' to finish.

Once, my mother gave me two pence at dinner time to go and buy some cakes for the party. I was over the moon! My ego was boosted no end! I would sit with the exalted that day and eat. I went to Westons at the top of Hampstead Road and looked into the glass-fronted biscuit tins. My eyes settled on the biggest, round, puff-pastry affairs with a hollow in the centre. Mother, when I showed them to her, said it was for jam but, jam or no jam, they were still cakes to me. There were six or seven, if I remember aright. After dinner, I proudly gave the nun the paper bag of cakes, then took my place at the desk with great expectancy. This was going to be a red letter day.

'Everyone who's brought something,' she called when we'd settled down, 'can come to the front now for the party.' I joined the elect and went forward to take one of the little seats formed in a circle. Unfortunately, there's many a fall awaiting the unwary. The nun stopped me on the way. 'You can't join the party,' she said, holding out her cane to bar my way, 'you were absent from school one day this week.' To say I was crestfallen would be the understatement of the year. I seemed fated to miss out on the eats and always be a spectator at the banquet. As I watched others tucking in to the cakes, mine included, I remember, as I said before, feeling sorry for my mother who'd parted with tuppence for nothing.

The Bishop's visit

The Bishop of the diocese visited the convent while I was there. It was a great event and after intercession by the Reverend Mother we children were to be allowed to kiss his ring. The instructions were that we genuflected, then mounted the steps and after kneeling and kissing the Bishop's ring, picked up a packet of sweets that would be by his side. We were eventually lined up and entered his presence singly. I entered the room when my turn came. The Bishop, surrounded by nuns, sat in state on a dais covered with a magnificent tasselled canopy of red velvet. His hand rested on his knee, exposing the amethyst stone set in a jewelled ring. I genuflected, mounted the three steps, knelt down and then events happened with such rapidity that must have bewildered even the Bishop; for when I knelt down and beheld the pile of sweets in conical bags, I completely forgot about the Bishop, the ecclesiastical ritual, the Holy Catholic Church and just grabbed one of the bags of sweets.

The effect was electrical. I was immediately seized by two nuns. The sweets were snatched from my hand, my head gently pressed down to reverently kiss the amethyst and I was then removed from the august presence with, to say the least, the minimum of ceremony. They weren't standing any nonsense from a little five-year-old heretic like me! Later, my sister found me crying in one of the corridors and when I'd related my tale of woe, she said she would try to get some sweets for me. Whether her appeal was successful or not I cannot recall, but I think I eventually got a handful of sweets.

Council school

Seven was the age limit for boys at the convent but I was expelled at the ripe old age of six. What with being a 'flasher', a 'messer' and a heretic into the bargain, the nuns had had a bellyful of me.

Life at the council school, where I went next, wasn't much different from the convent. It was rule by the rod, regardless, and every child was called by his or her surname. It was Wilson this or Crone that and if you were guilty of noisily dropping a hinged seat, a pencil or a slate, a caning on the hand was the result. In the infants, the teacher had a stick about a yard long, thick at the butt end and tapering to a diameter of about half an inch. This was far more cruel as a weapon than the leather straps used in the juniors and seniors, for there was no give in it. Indeed the only give was in the tender flesh of the infant.

After receiving the cane, our palms used to swell with frightful pain, then go numb for nearly an hour. During this period, it was impossible to grip, let alone write, with pencil or crayon. When the intense pain returned, it was a sign that your hand was getting better. Imagine! We were continually brainwashed by the teachers to believe that our school was one of the better schools — God help the kids in the worst.

In the juniors, I remember well an uproar that absolutely froze me with horror. One morning a girl was hauled out in front of the class and asked why she hadn't answered two teachers who called out to her as she left school on the previous Friday afternoon. What they wanted her for I didn't know, but the girl denied hearing them call. The other woman teacher was brought in to corroborate what ours had said and both eventually shouted at the girl, calling her a liar. At the child's repeated denials, they became more and more incensed, until both of them were hitting her across the shoulders and back with the straps. The girl by now had become really terrified and started screaming and shouting for her elder sister, who was in another class across the school hall.

'Janet, Janet, help me,' she screamed, 'Janet, Janet, help me.' Then we heard a commotion outside the classroom door. It was the child's sister who had heard the pitiful appeal from her classroom and had rushed out, regardless of the consequences, to help. We could hear scuffling outside as she

fought, trying to get in, and her heartrending pleading, 'Hit me instead of her. Please hit me instead of her.' I cannot remember how it ended, but my heart was frozen with horror and pity for the two sisters.

Another episode concerned a boy treating numerous school pals to sweets. For a boy to treat several pals at a time was an unheard of luxury, as we seldom received money to spend. At the odd times we did, we had to spend wisely. When I was given a halfpenny on Saturday, I used to eye the sweets with longing, but bought an apple or something else instead, because of fear of the wrath to come. Twice, Alan Seymour bought me a sherbet dab — other boys plonked for toffee apples, liquorice allsorts, lucky horseshoes, unclaimed babies and so on. Never before had we known such affluence and wanton luxury.

Alas, paradise cannot last long on this earth. The fall was bound to come — and it did. One afternoon as we filed into class a woman was talking to the teacher and headmaster. It turned out that the sorrowful woman had been the unwilling party to our debauchery, for son Alan had been pinching money from her purse. Then about fifteen of us were lined up in front of the class and each one told to confess what he had been given. I was about the least evil with two sherbet dabs to my discredit. Some of the felons must have nearly destocked the tuck shop. One boy had as many as three bottles of lemonade. 'Do you realise,' said the weeping mother, between sobs, 'that all your names will be written down in God's book — for ever! From now on, you are all condemned in the sight of God.' After a few more sobs, she repeated with emphasis, 'For ever!' How we were to know that the money had been stolen, beats me. We all had two straps on each hand from the headmaster after a lengthy lecture on our present depraved state, but no one was deported to Australia, so our school must have been one of the best. On Judgement Day, I'll invite the Lord to a sherbet dab. It might shorten my penance!

The Farndale Rovers

We decided to form a football club and call ourselves The Farndale Rovers. My two friends George Archibald and Conley Slater, along with me, had long cherished the idea of forming a team. The pitch would be in the back lane and we'd muster other lads who lived above the opening, then take on all comers. The 'opening' was a gap in our street where some said two builders, starting from different sides of the street, had stopped building. The space left, sufficient to build a house on, came in handy for the local children, because we could play cricket or rounders, skipping for the girls, and in the dark evenings of winter the bigger kids did a spot of covert courting. Incandescent candles had just come in and one, on a lamp in the lane, shone into the opening. Some of the daring lads in Standard Seven had been known to climb the lamp post and break the mantle so that their love affairs couldn't be seen.

If we were to start a football team, a football was an obvious necessity and the best way to raise funds to buy one was, we agreed, to start by giving a party and concert in one of our backyards. My backyard was no good because the butcher sometimes used it for cleaning the tripe and sausage skins. Conley Slater's mother said we could use her backyard, 'providing we behaved ourselves.' I, being fairly good at writing, was to print out a sheet of paper to tack on the back door, with the time and attractions of the event. It was to be headed 'The Farndale Rovers'. My brother Walter promised to get some stale cakes cheap from Mrs Robinson's bakery and grocery shop, where he ran errands and delivered for fourpence a week. The social entertainment was to be provided by me in Mrs Slater's up-turned poss-tub, pretending to be a gramophone.

On the Friday night, a week prior to the event, I started printing out the notice with black crayon on a sheet of my school exercise book. I knew how to spell 'Farndale' because we were at the top of that road, but when I got to the word 'Rovers', I wasn't sure how it was spelt. My eldest brother, Charlie, was busy washing the dishes in the scullery, so I called out to him. 'Charlie, how do you spell "rovers"?' There was silence for a while, then he called back, 'r-u-f-f-e-r-s'. When I'd laboriously printed it out, it didn't look right to me, but not wanting to highlight my ignorance and to receive ridicule, I remained silent. And so, on the following Monday night, the following notice was tacked onto Mrs Slater's back door: 'THE FARNDALE RUFFERS. ON SATURDAY AT 2 O'CLOCK. A GRAND PARTY HERE. HALF-PENNY TO GET IN AND A CAKE.'

We spread the news to all and sundry during the week and on Friday night, after delivering the groceries, my brother brought the stale cakes home. He'd paid a penny for them. They weren't only stale, they were so broken and mixed up that bits of jam tarts had to be prized from the rock buns and three old tea cakes were showing cracks like parched mud after a phenomenal drought. I think the matching up of the jam tarts and custard tarts was the first jigsaw puzzle we did. Bits that didn't fit anywhere were eaten.

Saturday arrived. Sixteen patched up cakes were laid out on a newspaper on the lavatory seat — it was the wooden wall-to-wall kind. The three of us stood at the back door to collect the money and make sure there were no gate crashers. As each one parted with his or her ha'penny they were told to go into the lavatory and pick a cake. Now being novices at this type of fund raising, we didn't take the necessary precautions to allow for the frailty of human nature. After a lot of pushing and shoving, six had got in and were evidently satisfied, but the seventh came back from the lavatory and said there were no cakes left. Not only did he say there were no cakes left, but he said he'd tell the 'pollis' if he didn't get his ha'penny back. The half dozen still waiting to get in, hearing that all the cakes had gone, started arguing that it was against the law to charge for a party anyway and we could be had up before the beak. This confrontation immediately turned us weak at the knees, because Peggy Sproat was already in the backyard and her dad *was* a pollis! Truth to tell, she'd had her money's worth, for I remember she had a lump of tea cake in her hand, yet her mouth was jammy. Now all the cakes had gone and with the threat of the law hanging over our heads, the rest were allowed in free.

To take their minds off the money and with a diplomacy remarkable for our age, we launched straight into the entertainment part of the afternoon. My two pals turned the poss-tub upside down with me inside armed with a hammer; for my act was to sing and then pretend, at frequent intervals, that the motor had broken down.

'Now,' shouted my pal Georgie, above the din, 'what would you like the gramophone to play?'

A chorus of suggestions were called. I heard one shouting 'John Brown's Body' and I knew this. I started my act.

'This is an Edison Bell record,' I squeaked out, 'and I will now sing John Brown's Body.' 'John Brown's body lies amouldrin' in the grave. John Brown's body lies amouldrin' in the grave. John Brown's body lies am-o-u—l—d—-r—i——n'. At this point I started giving 'raspberries' and banging the side of the tub with a hammer. The effect on the listeners was electric. They went into hysterical laughter. The gramophone speeded up again: 'i——n—t-h-e grave and his soul goes marchin' on. Glory, Glory, Halle-l—u—-j—-a——h.' Bang, clatter, wallop! The motor had broken down again. I found that by hitting the top of the tub, it made more noise and the louder the bangs, the better the audience liked it. The singing left them stone cold. It was the banging and farting going on inside the tub that sent them into hysterical laughter. This entertainment was going down well. 'Let some air in!' I would shout now and again, for I was getting suffocated. Willing hands would tip the tub up while I gasped in fresh air, then the fun started again. It wasn't only the ones outside the tub that were enjoying it, I was having a whale of a time myself.

Now at that age, I wasn't conversant with the laws of resistance in the structure of different substances — that when iron is battered against wood, the wood of necessity gives way to the iron. As I belted away with the hammer during the rendering of 'Annie Laurie', suddenly there was a splintering of wood and the hammer went straight through the tub.

As if by magic, dead silence fell on the audience, then things happened in rapid succession. I heard Mrs Slater come out, demanding in a shrill voice what all the noise was about and simultaneously the back door opened and I heard the audience scattering up and down the back lane. It was all right for them, but I was left trapped inside the tub. She must have seen the hammer as I wriggled it vigorously, trying to get it back. 'Who's that inside my tub?' She tipped the tub onto its side. I crawled out backwards and made a run for the open door, but wasn't fast enough. She grabbed me by the hair and started shaking me as if I were a rag doll.

'What have you done to my tub? Do you see you've broken my tub!' Each admonition was accompanied by a shake. My eyes were watering, but I remained mute. 'Who's going to pay for my tub?'

Her voice now had the ring of despair. Suddenly, she released her grip on my hair and, as I ran for the door and freedom, got a stinging smack across the ear which sent me reeling against the jamb. As I ran up the deserted lane, she called after me,'Your mother will have to pay for this.' I cannot remember if my mother was told about this, but it's not surprising that the woman was really vexed, because to buy a new poss-tub in those days must have been a major expense on a very meagre income. As I say, I cannot recall how it ended, but I do know that Farndale Ruffers were never heard of again.

Street brawls

Our street was a place of upheaval and I felt a foreboding feeling in the atmosphere. I had a subconscious conviction that marriage was the greatest tragedy which could befall anyone. Later in life, everyone has a chance of a partner at some time or other and usually feels apprehensive of the permanent change in their life. With me, it wasn't just apprehension, it was stark terror. Certainly I liked the company of the opposite sex, but as to getting married — never! Because of my reactions, I think some of my lady loves thought that there must be some physical impediment stopping me from taking the plunge; for directly a relationship seemed to blossom into permanency, I became like a petrified rabbit. The cause was the regular sight of couples fighting in the street.

Saturday and Sunday nights were the high time of the week for brawls. Couples would be battling it out in the streets. Why they went outside, God alone knows. The argument, often over the most trivial matter, would start in the house, swaying one way then the other and gaining in momentum until the couple ended outside the front door. Usually, half a dozen onlookers from the pubs would stand around enjoying free entertainment, but if the fight they were watching was losing some of its gusto, they would run down the street to watch another where more sparks were flying.

Some of us sought solace in religion — a form of escapism I suppose, but it seemed to me that the harder I prayed the louder people seemed to shout and fight, so I gave it up as a bad job. My youngest sister was terribly timid and nervous and, still being at the convent school, continued to seek comfort in prayer. Once I kneeled behind her in church and with head bent in intense prayer, from my position, I had the impression that her body had completely departed and left only an empty coat. It's not surprising that we were all highly strung throughout life, for the early turmoil and environment had a lasting effect. Restlessness and migraine headaches were permanent states in our later life and I had a fear of being indoors, yet our house wasn't considered unusual in our neighbourhood.

Later, when I started to apply a little of my own logic, it became apparent that there was something radically wrong. For one thing, I was surprised to learn that all couples didn't fight and that in the countryside amongst the cattle there was a peace beyond understanding. Animals in the fields and their young seemed more placid and therefore more logical than humans. The lambs and calves gambolled and played with unrestrained joy. Indeed, to them life appeared a constant source of love and joy — living for living's sake. My earliest thoughts indicated that the tongue is the source of all evil, but the tongue merely utters what the mind thinks; so what makes the mind turn to good or evil? Christianity has been with us for about two thousand years, yet the animals in the fields seem to be closer to Christian ideals than people. It must be something deeper than an affirmation of principle. Some fundamental motive force must have caused humans to lose their way.

The clairvoyant

My mother used to invite friends and relatives to the house for a party and, being war time, everyone brought something to eat, while a clairvoyant was engaged to come and gaze into the crystal ball. After the meal, she would sit in one of the attic rooms that had been specially prepared. A red glass bowl covered the gas mantle which was turned low. Curtains or blankets were hung to form a small cubicle and every client paid sixpence to find out what life had in store for them. My father wouldn't go in because sixpence was good beer money, plus the fact that I think he was a bit scared of it all. 'Damned Tommy rot,' he used to say, 'the woman shouldn't be allowed in the house. I don't know why the woman's invited.' However, once, he was persuaded to go in. Mrs Bulman, an old friend of the family, accused him of being frightened, an accusation that he flatly denied. 'Right,' she added, pursuing the point she had gained, 'if I pay the sixpence, will you go in?' This unwelcome generosity left no loophole. He had to risk it.

Now the routine was that as each one came out of the attic, they came downstairs and related to a huddled group in the sitting room all that the crystal-gazer had told them. When my father came down, it was obvious even to me that he'd had a mighty big shock. He was agitated and ill at ease, quite unusual for him. When one or two tentatively asked him what she had said, he was evasive. 'Those people shouldn't be brought into the house. Meddlin' with spirits was never meant.' Everyone could see he was disturbed and regretted going in. 'It's wrong to meddle with such things,' I remember him saying as a sort of summing up remark.

My mother had gone in after him. I was sitting on a stool in a corner of the fireplace with eyes, ears and mouth all wide open, listening and fascinated by the sequence of events. Eventually, my mother came down from the attic. As she entered the room everyone looked at her expectantly. Instead of my father's reticence putting them off, it had whetted their curiosity; perhaps the clairvoyant had told her some juicy forecast.

'What did she say, Jenny? She kept you a long time. Was she good?'

'Oh, nothing startling,' replied my mother in an off-hand way. 'Just to watch this and watch that and the good news is that a present is coming from an unexpected quarter.'

Even I wasn't bluffed, she'd been with the fortune-teller for nearly half an hour yet what she'd told us, or rather them, for I wasn't supposed to be there, could have been told and embellished upon in five minutes. My father listened apprehensively, then left to go into the kitchen where he used to sit in front of the fire smoking his clay pipe. He seemed to sense that something was being withheld and that his company wasn't wanted. A dead silence fell on the company: everyone looked at my mother again expectantly. She waited in silence until she heard the kitchen door close — then dropped the bombshell.

'I'm going to lose my husband!'

All the listeners became frozen as statues in their various positions. This was drama. This was tragedy. This was dynamite. And all for sixpence! Everyone waited with baited breath for her to continue.

'Yes, as soon as I sat down, she took both my hands in hers and said, "Jenny, I've bad news for you. I saw it in the crystal as soon as Charlie came in. I'm sorry to have to tell you this, but he has an incurable disease and his death will be slow." '

The atmosphere in the room was tense. No one spoke. All eyes and attention were on my mother, waiting for more.

'He'll go into hospital soon, probably within a month,' she said, 'and he'll be in and out most of the time for two or three years, and while he's home I'll have a lot of nursing jobs to do.' She went on and on giving more details and information of what lay ahead, until even the most insatiable of her spellbound audience were satisfied.

Prophesy comes true

All the prophesies about my father came true. After the operation, my father was in and out of the hospital for three years before he died, just as the clairvoyant had predicted. Whether she had told him anything about his impending doom, I cannot say, but I believe that depressing information of this nature is not normally passed on to a client. However, she must at least have hinted at something for he was obviously shaken after the interview.

They brought his body home from the workhouse where he'd spent his last days and he was laid out in the front room.

During his illness he suffered dreadful pain and moaned periodically through the nights, but the relationship had always been a depressing one. While the body was laid out in the front room, my brothers and eldest sister went into town to see about the formalities for the burial. My youngest sister was left to clean the house and I went out on the bike. When I returned, she was washing the dishes in the scullery. I had a feeling she was nervous and glad to see someone. She looked at me with startled eyes, like someone who has seen a ghost. 'While you were out, I heard Dad say "Bessie" quite plainly!'

No wonder she was hearing things. A little girl left on her own with a corpse!

The funeral

The funeral was also a strange affair. All our in-laws and out-laws came. Uncle Joe on my father's side with his three daughters, Charlotte, Ruby and Dora. Aunt Alice and her husband Dave. Mrs Winter, an old friend of the family who always fascinated us children, for she was enormously fat and absorbed in spiritualism. She would relate to us hair-raising stories about knockings, warnings about disasters, of curses, of death, and she was the most naturally gifted orator I have ever known. How she ever grew so fat was a mystery to me, for one slice of bread and margarine would last her all tea time. She would placidly and dramatically narrate a ghostly experience and suddenly stop just when you wanted her to go on. Then she would take a small bite of bread, slowly and deliberately masticate it, then start again. It's amazing how stories of contact with the astral world always held a fascination, even from our earliest years. Sometimes my mother used to go with Mrs Winter to spiritualist meetings.

After my father's death, Mrs. Winter implored her to go to a meeting. 'Charlie's bound to have a message,' she kept saying.

After a lot of persuasion my mother went. The medium soon picked her out. I felt sorry for the medium — she didn't know my mother.

'Have you lost someone very close lately?'

'Yes.'

'I see a middle aged man and he has a message for you.'

No answer.

'It looks like a man that could have been your husband.'

No answer.

'Have you recently lost your husband?'

'Yes, I have.'

'Well, he has a message for you.'

My mother wanted more information to make sure she wasn't hobnobbing with a strange man.

'Could you tell me what he looks like?'

'Well, he appears to be of medium height, broad, fifty-ish.'

'Could you tell me the colour of his hair?' asked my mother.

Now this was a real crafty question, because my father was as bald as a billiard ball — a real Kojak. But when you get two crafty women trying to get the ascendancy over each other, it's a case of 'Greek meets Greek'. My mother said the medium hesitated and then answered, 'I cannot see. He has his hat on.' Which I think was a clever answer to an acute question.

'No,' she replied, 'I don't know him.'

During this exchange, Mattie Winter kept nudging my mother, whispering, 'Jenny, it's Charlie.' But evidently my mother wouldn't be nudged into submission.

At the funeral I sat in the second horse-drawn carriage with my elder brother, my sister and another relation, Sarah McGregor. Sarah, by the way, had risen in the world by one big bound, for she had worked in a kitchen and provided meals from six in the morning till late at night for some ten hauliers who worked for her employer. He owned heavy draught horses that used to be hitched onto carts in front of the shaft horses at the wharf to help haul heavy loads from the River Tyne up into the town. At the top of Dean Street, they were unhitched and repeated the pulling from the wharf all over again. Sarah was the one and only cook and ruled the men with a rod of iron. She had the build and stance of a female all-in wrestler — head aggressively jutting forward, arms slightly raised from the sides, as if permanently prepared to tackle any opposition, and a tongue that could lash anyone into submission.

But Sarah didn't just cook, for while she stirred the dixies of porridge and sweated over huge pots of stew, she schemed; and eventually her scheming brought dividends, for she married the boss and then ruled him with a rod of iron. A more oddly matched couple would have been hard to find, for she was short, squat and aggressive, whereas he was tall, thin and studious. Being slightly deaf, he held his head to one side and always appeared to be listening for the final call — which, being married to Sarah, he probably was.

It rained dismally all the way to the cemetery. Sarah was in black from head to foot and frequently gave a mighty sigh before breaking the silence, saying in the gloomy carriage, 'Happy are the dead that the rain falls on.' We sat quietly and resigned, the only sound being the squeaking and rumbling of the carriage wheels and the metallic clinking of the horses' hooves on the cobblestones. Then another sigh would issue from the gloom, 'Happy are the dead that the rain falls on.'

My father was buried in Elswick cemetery. I watched the burial quite detached and unmoved. After the burial, we went back to the house for a meal. While everyone ate potted meat sandwiches and cheese with pickled onions, Father's relatives seemed to be wanting to air a few grievances. Children are sensitive to the atmosphere and I could detect a cloaked hostility in the air.

'Ay, he died in the workhouse, poor man,' sighed Uncle Joe, breaking the silence. Really, I think he died in a part of the workhouse reserved for the treatment of incurables.

'That clock should have been stopped,' said Uncle George, looking reproachfully at our three and sixpenny alarm clock ticking cheekily away on the mantlepiece.

'Yes, and that grandfather clock in the passage should have been covered with a black cloth too,' added Dora Bell, getting an extra dig in while the going was good.

'Ah, the poor man never missed a day's work in his life,' said David Fenwick, wiping his eyes with a white spotted red handkerchief.

'And never appreciated either,' added Ruby Bell, after a pregnant silence.

The communal sighs and crunching of pickled onions continued.

'Yes, died in the workhouse,' sighed Uncle Joe again.

Anyway, at two o'clock there was a general exodus. The pubs closed at half past.

A good father

Uncle Joe was a good man though; over six feet tall, very broad and his three daughters thought the world of him. My cousin Charlotte often told me later about their childhood and how their father looked after them. He never argued or drank too much. Her mother would taunt her husband about the children. 'Those girls of yours run wild in the streets. You've got no control over them. What they'll grow up like, God alone knows. Spare the rod and spoil the child, that's you. Too soft, that's your trouble. I've got to be a mother and father to those girls,' and so she would go on and on. In the end, for the sake of peace, Charlotte said her dad would pick up a cane, look sternly at them, point to the door and say, 'Dora, Charlotte, Ruby, go into the other room,' then he followed them in. 'Now,' he would say, 'Howl your heads off!' and while he shouted as they yelled, the row was enough to convince their mother that chastisement was being meted out.

Cause and effect

I consider now that fighting parents were in no way to blame for their behaviour. They were puppets dancing to the tune of a discordant world. Products of centuries of wars, killing, diseases, drinking, viciousness — everything negative and nasty that could be conjured up. Had they and their forebears been nurtured in an atmosphere more akin to the original, the Garden of Eden, they would have reflected a similar peaceful nature and tranquillity. For cause and effect applies to everything and the effect is in no way to blame — only the cause, for effect is the unavoidable sequence. Plant a perfect potato in poor, pest-ridden soil and it will produce a grub-eaten warty tuber. Now plant this tuber to produce again in the same poor soil and its tuber will be even worse. The result is still a potato, true to specie, but both environmental circumstances and heredity have had a combined detrimental effect and it is now a sorry specimen of the original. Until both these conditions are changed, improvement is just wishful thinking.

Exactly the same rule applies to humans, for the law of cause and effect exists in all creation, from the lowest form of life to the highest, the simplest to the most complex. Man's mind has become, through generations of wrong eating habits leading to wrong thinking, his own biggest enemy. Within the cage of his head, constant thoughts of fear, frustration, aggression, depression and negative reactions to outside influences revolve until he dies; a bundle of self-imposed complexes all built up from a misguided but habitual way of life.

There is no doubt that different foods dictate the behaviour of the eater. Compare the nature of the carnivore with that of the herbivore. The former is aggressive, the latter peaceful. Watch the predatory animal go in for the kill. It builds up a frenzy of hate to achieve its purpose

Is it not logical to infer that this basic aggression must also be smouldering in the flesh-eating human? Although we pride ourselves on being civilised and humane by dispatching our victims instantly, the primordial and barbaric instinct to kill remains. There is no other explanation for the viciousness prevalent today. Faith in deities and religion may suppress this evil in man, but only a reformed diet will eradicate it. There are universal laws to which we must adhere, for the basis of all being is to ride on a wave of harmony which transmits and receives in a vast cosmic circle. If we bring our lives as far as possible in line with this harmony, we are bound to benefit. If we create discord by killing for meat and inflict suffering by eating dairy produce, then we are bound to suffer in return, for the original code of Eden has been broken. The basic cause of adverse conditions, both in the spiritual and physical life, is a direct result of the wrong food on our table. For how can we hope to advance in harmony and peace, yet continue to be predatory animals at the same time?

Starting work

After leaving school, I got a job at a Liberal Club. The wage was four shillings (20p) a week plus food. I worked with another page boy from 7.30 in the morning until 5 o'clock one week and to 9 o'clock the next week. In the morning we cleaned windows and brasses, ran errands and made ourselves generally useful. In the afternoon we worked in the billiard room, marking the players' scores on a board. After nine o'clock, Mr Geeson, the old attendant in charge, looked after one table while the other players had to mark their own scores. Sometimes he would have a heart attack and sit slumped in a wooden easy chair for about half an hour, then slowly recover. I often thought he was going to die.

When he was off work because of illness, whoever was on the late shift that week had to work until ten and was in charge of the till. When the players paid, I had to fill in a slip with the names of the members and the time the table was occupied. When all members had left, I would have the nightmare task of reckoning up the money. The money in the till never tallied with the amount I should have according to the slips. It was always short. Money and slips were then put into a leather bag and dropped through a large letter box in the cashier's office. Next morning I was called to the office and told that the money was short. Of course this wasn't news to me. At odd times, when the money tallied, I would still be called to the office to try and account for the shortage.

Two things puzzled me. One was that I knew I was good at arithmetic at school, so I wasn't wrong in the reckoning. The other thing was that I never got the sack! Suddenly it dawned on me — the place was a den of pilfering.

When I was on late duty, one or two of the servants would come up from the dining room and help themselves to a half-crown or change a note from the till while I was engaged at one of the tables. This was a loophole hard to close because I couldn't leave the table at which I was marking and if I gave a frantic sign for them to wait, they would indicate that a member was waiting downstairs and open the till regardless. They weren't the only ones pinching. If no one had been for change and the cash was right, I would cycle back home tired but happy. Yet I would still be called to the cashier's office next morning to be told that the cash was short. There was only one answer. The young woman treasurer wasn't averse to a little boost to her wages either. Once they sent the hall porter to the bank to change twenty pounds into small silver. They're still waiting for him to return.

Communication throughout the club was by tube. To use it you had to remove the whistle and blow down the tube to blow the whistle at the other end. The number of whistles denoted the department. Then you put your ear to the tube to make sure someone was there, then shouted the order.

Once, a member asked me to order him two Benedictines. I blew down the tube twice for the dining room, then shouted, 'Two Benedictines,' then I put my ear to the tube.

'What?' shouted back the girl at the other end.

'Two Benedictines, please,' I yelled down the tube again.

'Two what?'

'Two Benedictines!' I shouted down the tube again, then had to leave and get on marking at a table.

Soon the servant came upstairs to the billiard room and asked why someone wanted two bully-beef tins!

We used to go down to the kitchen for meals, supper was at 7.30 and the cook would often have fish and chips ready, but the fish had to be the cheapest and the manageress often came down to see what we were eating. However she was on the fiddle as well, because when a whole fresh salmon or cod was ordered for the club, I always had the job of taking the best centre-cut to her private house. Another errand I had was to go to the grocers who supplied the club and ask for the 'staff bacon'. This used to be cut on the slicer from the boned scrag ends.

I left the club and got an apprenticeship at a large store in the centre of the city. Although the wage was now seven shillings and sixpence (37p), I was worse off because there was no food supplied and I had to wear a dark suit, white collar and black tie. At the club the page boy's uniform had been supplied free. My father had died, so I had four inches cut off the legs of a dark grey suit he left and wore that.

All transactions at the store were by 'tin money' called 'Tokens'. Agents around the town and neighbouring villages, usually women, gave out these credit tokens then collected a small profit from both the shop and the customer. The store ran no risk of bad debts because each agent was responsible for her own particular borrowers. Really, the apprenticeship scheme was eyewash, just a ruse for cheap labour. Each year twenty youngsters were medically examined, then given a big important-looking printed sheet of paper with a red embossed stamp and three flourishing signatures at the bottom. The apprenticeship was for three years and if you were lucky — very lucky — after the three years you might be kept on, but the bulk were fired and another batch of youngsters started. One person supervised about half a dozen of us and we spent six months in each department: furnishing, clothing, bedding, linen, etc. Really the two men who owned the store couldn't be blamed for these tactics because the depression in those days was terrible and it must have been an uphill job for them, trying to scrape a little profit.

The call of the Outback

Soon, I realised that the present prospects were nil and with over three million out of work the labour landscape in England looked bleak. There were, at that time, adverts in the papers holding forth on the golden opportunities for youth in Australia, 'The Land of Sunshine'. Brightly coloured hoardings showed a drove of sheep grazing on sun drenched pasture land with a sun tanned drover sitting on horseback in the foreground.

The call of the outback struck. I applied for an assisted passage out to the land of sunshine and promise. I was told to attend the Australian Agent's office in Newcastle for an interview and medical inspection. I took the day off work and went. After a short interview about my reason for wanting to go to the dominion, I joined fifteen other prospective emigrants and was given a lecture on the kind of life and work to expect, then we stood in line ready for the 'medical'. A man in a lounge suit came in, walked along the line, giving each in turn a dig in the solar plexus with his fist. Those who didn't drop down dead were O.K. When I didn't return to the store, they wrote threatening me with a fine if I didn't complete my apprenticeship. I was hoping they'd deport me to Australia, it would have come in handy and saved me the sixteen pounds that I promised to pay back the immigration people when I got work in the far-off land.

LIFE IN THE LAND OF SUNSHINE

I N NOVEMBER 1928, along with three hundred and sixty other hopefuls, I sailed from Tilbury Docks, London for Perth, Australia on the SS *Berrima* — an old tub of a vessel that some said had been salvaged twice during the 1914-18 war. It pitched and tossed in the slightest swell through being so wide. There were four of us in our cabin and going through the Bay of Biscay we all lay on our bunks like wet dish-rags through the sea-sickness, while trunks slid from one end of the cabin to the other with the heavy rolling of the ship. One emigrant had been a fisherman on the trawlers in Scotland and he told us that one morning he had been the only one in the saloon for breakfast.

Iron bulkhead doors slammed, chains rattled, passengers shouted and when you went for a wash at the stern, water on the steel floor sloshed from side to side. During the voyage, I met a man who stuttered so badly that it was actually embarrassing waiting for him to get a word out. One day, I was surprised to see his name on the notice board as one of the singers in a concert party. I purposely went along to the show to hear him and was amazed. He sang a song, then an encore, perfectly without hesitation.

We called in at the Canary Islands and, from the deck of the ship, the land I could see in the distance looked like paradise after smoky old Newcastle. One or two boats came out with bananas. They were small, deep yellow and tasted delicious. After we left the islands, the ocean, in complete contrast to the Bay of Biscay, was now dead calm and in the brilliant sunshine reminded me of burnished crocodile leather — flat, yet with a myriad dapples winking in the sunlight. The brilliant light caused sun-glare and for a few days I could scarcely open my eyes on deck.

We arrived at Cape Town on a Sunday morning. In the evening, I went with some shipmates into the Government House Gardens. When it got dark, a lot of the trees were suddenly lit up with coloured electric bulbs. The immediate effect was one of fairyland, and the warm tropical air, in contrast to the cold and gloom of home, completed the atmosphere of enchantment. At this time, being young and impressionable and having read the adventures of

Marco Polo and other explorers, I was in that frame of mind when I imagined any bizarre event was likely to unfold. If I'd seen a row of pink elephants dancing the can-can, I wouldn't have been unduly surprised.

Arrival

After leaving the Cape and crossing the Indian Ocean, where we saw flying fishes and dolphins curving out of the water and sharks scavenging the refuse thrown out from the galley, we went on to Perth in Western Australia.

The heat, after the ship had tied up at the wharf, was stifling, like an oven. I felt suffocated. An Australian woman came on board, probably to meet an immigrant and we remarked on the heat. 'Oh,'she replied, 'this isn't a particularly hot day for Australia.' I got scared. I thought 'I'll never get used to this heat' but it's amazing how quickly the body adjusts to new conditions, for within a few days this initial fear of suffocation had left me. The Immigration Officer came on board and although each immigrant was supposed to have a job awaiting him, this was far from so. We had come out under various schemes and about twenty of us seemed to have come out the worst as far as jobs were considered. To make matters worse, knowing we had little or no money, none of the hotels or boarding houses would take us, so we stayed on board and picked out of a hat for the jobs as they came in.

Getting a job

On the fourth day I was lucky and picked a job at a place called Karridale, in the South-West. I was given a rail pass and told my new boss would meet me at the siding. This proved to be more wishful thinking than fact; for after travelling through miles of forest, I was dumped onto a small wooden platform in the heart of the bush and the train steamed away, leaving me with my bundle of belongings in the middle of nowhere with not a soul or shack in sight. After an hour or so, it started to get dark and as there was no sign of life, I decided to set off along the track and look for any habitation.

I was just picking up my bundle when I heard the sound of a truck approaching. Within seconds and in a swirling cloud of dust, an old Ford appeared and came to a halt beside the platform. A gaunt, studious looking man got out and started to unload boxes. For all the notice he took of me, I could have been invisible. I asked him if he knew a Mr Richardson. 'Bill Richardson? Yes,' he drawled, while he continued to unload.

'Will he be coming to the siding?'

'No. Never does. You an immigrant?'

'Yes. He was supposed to meet me at the siding. I'm going to work for him.'

He took the last couple of boxes off the truck in silence, studiously got a tin of tobacco and papers from his pocket, rolled himself a cigarette and after taking a couple of inhalations, spoke words of profound wisdom. 'Probably didn't get the letter.'

I watched with a feeling of apprehension as he went to the front of the truck and got in again, but much to my relief he opened the opposite door and called out, 'Jump in!' I didn't need a second invitation and as I got into the seat I felt relieved that I had, at least, contacted another human. 'I'll put you up for the night and take you out to Bill Richardson's place in the morning,' he shouted above the din of the motor as he revved up. And so, in a cloud of dust, we were off. It turned out he was the local store keeper, and behind his detached manner he was really quite friendly. He and his wife fixed me up for the night with, as I found out later, the hospitality typical of Australians and next day I was taken out to my first job in the land of sunshine and promise.

Clearing the bush

The storekeeper was right. Bill Richardson hadn't received a letter about my arrival from the Immigration Office. It arrived a week after me. He also was an immigrant, having been in the country some ten years. He lived in a wooden bungalow with his wife and three children, and was busy clearing the surrounding bush of trees and undergrowth under the guidance and payment by a government foreman.

The government scheme I helped him to work was good, but unfortunately abused by some of the settlers. Each settler was given 150 acres of bush country with a wooden bungalow, horse and cart and all the necessary tools for clearing the land. As soon as a couple of acres were cleared, he was supplied with clover seed and, as soon as this had grown, he got a cow for domestic purposes. Originally, they had also been given a young boar and sow with which to start breeding. This had been stopped because some settlers promptly killed the pigs and ate them. When the government foreman called he was told that the pigs had died, escaped into the bush, or any other plausible excuse that came to mind. The scheme was finalised when the settler had enough land under clover to support a herd of twenty cows. Now that the holding was a self-supporting unit, government valuers would visit the farm and assess its value, regardless of the money put into it. Suppose they valued it at two thousand pounds, then the settler was now on his own and had to pay 7% a year back to the government on that assessment. Hence, on two thousand pounds he had a yearly bill of one hundred and forty pounds, plus the option of eventually owning the farm by paying off the capital in instalments. Some of the earlier settlers had nice little dairy farms and sent the cream into Busselton to be made into butter for export. At the new location I was on, clearing the virgin bush was hard work; ringbarking the large jarrah and red gums, chopping down the smaller trees and grubbing up the scrub between with a mattock. Being in the shade of the trees while working was often a respite from the pitiless sun, but the heat was still blistering and a peculiar sweet, yet decaying scent of the bush pervaded the air.

The domestic scene, however, didn't differ much from the life I'd known in England. For the couple I was with either weren't on speaking terms or were fighting and arguing. Bread and dripping were the staple diet and orange boxes provided most of the furniture. Sometimes Mrs Richardson made a treacle pudding, but it was so solid I preferred the treacle on bread. I slept in an outhouse and earned two pounds a month. One pound had to be sent to the government to pay for my fare out.

After I'd been there for six months, I woke up one Sunday morning to find the place deserted. They had packed everything onto the cart during the night and done a moonlight flit. Later in the day I walked through the bush to the government foreman's place and broke the news to him. He wasn't unduly surprised.

'Did he pay your wages up to date?' he asked.

I told him he owed me for the last month and had also borrowed a pound.

'Yes, and there's not only you,' he answered, 'he owes money all around the place and the horse and cart he's taken are government property too. Did he ever mention where he wanted to go?'

'No, never a word.'

The foreman fixed me up with a job clearing for a Mr Johnson, a much more reliable character and later, when I went in the sulky to the store for the rations, the storekeeper told me Mr Richardson owed him fifteen pounds. On the Sunday morning that my boss and his family had flown, he said he'd heard the creaking of wheels passing the store at about four in the morning and had wondered who it was. Probably that was why he was so offhand when I had mentioned my future employer's name at our first meeting at the siding. Probably he was owed money then. Another settler hadn't been paid for seven hens that he'd sold him. I remembered those hens which had accompanied Mr Richardson's belongings in his moonlight flit. They appeared ancient to me and during the six months I was there they never produced more than a couple of eggs a week. In fact, they were more of a liability than an asset.

Anyway, as I said, the foreman got me this job with Alan Johnson. He was still in the bush clearing stage but had two cows, a draught horse and cart, two hacks, a sulky and a nice five acre paddock of clover. He was also married with two daughters, was a good mixer and entertainer. He played the fiddle at the bush dances, while old Tom Steadman the farrier played the concertina, so he was very much in demand.

Shooting the wildlife

It was here I remember, that my first stab of conscience smote me about killing wildlife. It was whilst roaming the sunlit forest with two of my friends, one Sunday morning, that we spotted an iguana high up, lying along the branch of a redgum tree. Alex had a .22 rifle and fired at it a couple of times, but missed. Terry, his brother, tried but had no better luck. Being high up in the tree and with the bright sunlight dappling the leaves, the target wasn't easy. I tried my luck and after the second shot, we heard a gurgling, gasping sound. Terry shouted, 'It's bleeding at the throat.' We watched and listened as it gasped and bled, then suddenly it fell through the branches and lay dead at our feet. It was some four feet long with a shiny, scaly skin.

They are inoffensive, herbivorous creatures and that night, in bed, I kept thinking about this huge lizard and feeling horribly guilty. It had been enjoying the morning sunshine until we three trigger happy youths had appeared. I lay thinking, 'What good did that do? What senseless killing!' and similar remorseless thoughts. Lizards are queer creatures. They will remain for hours in an awkward pose with head raised sideways and then, quite suddenly, move with amazing speed.

Once I saw a huge jarrah tree lying on the ground with an iguana clinging motionless to the trunk. The tree had to be split with a gelignite charge for burning, for it is a very hard wood — some call it 'Australian mahogany'. The creature remained motionless as we auger drilled holes into the trunk, then packed down sticks of gelignite with fused detonators attached. We lit the fuses then ran for cover. From our vantage point we could still see the iguana in its characteristic pose, as if nothing had happened. Suddenly the silence was rent with a terrific explosion and as the dust billowed up from the detonations huge lumps of timber sailed through the air. One landed about ten feet from the foot of the tree behind which we were sheltering and, believe me, the huge lizard was still clinging to it in the same awkward pose, as if nothing had happened!

Another time I was trapping possum — a nocturnal fruit-eater. The method of trapping was to prop a long stick at an angle against a banksia tree which they frequent, and attached to the stick, a running noose about half way down. The possum climb up the trunk to eat the succulent blossom, but coming down it will take the easier way via the stick. It runs its head into the snare, the stick falls and it is trapped. Early one morning, going round the traps, I found two possum together lying in a bed of exotically scented 'donkey orchids', sound asleep at the base of the tree.

It was obvious what had happened, the doe possum had been caught and fought all through the night to free herself. Her fur was matted with perspiration and dust and, being half choked with the tight wire round her neck had eventually, with the coming of dawn, given up the struggle in exhaustion. Her offspring, a young buck, had come to sleep with her and there they lay, little furry arms around one another, lost in the oblivion of sleep. All this suffering and tragedy in their innocent lives to provide me with a shilling and a daft woman somewhere with an unnecessary fur coat. I hit them both together and although their deaths were swift and merciful, it finished my trapping days.

Courting days

It was at this time that Joyce Allen came into my life. We met at a dance in the schoolroom and the attraction seemed mutual. Her place was a mile or so from where I worked and both were connected by a track that meandered through the bush. Once, when I came in for dinner, Joyce had called to spend the day. Late at night we set off through the bush for her home and as we went through the dark wood, guided more by instinct than sight, she told me her real name was Joyce Wall. Her mother had married a second time and she was the daughter of the first marriage. As we went along, the croaking frogs chorused incessantly, an occasional bark from a wild dingo and the odd thumping of a kangaroo seemed to accentuate the surrounding silence and darkness. We were deep in conversation and completely oblivious to the rest of the world, when a man suddenly stepped out from behind a tree and held a lamp to our faces. It happened so quickly that I couldn't collect my wits. I just stood, being scrutinised. Joyce was quicker off the mark.

'How dare you spy on me?' she cried, stamping her foot.

'Oh, yes,' he said, ignoring the question, 'and who is this young pup?'

'That's none of your business,' she snapped back.

'Well,' I cut in, thinking it was high time I said something, 'I work for Mr Johnson and I'm seeing Joyce home.'

'Oh, and how old are you?' he demanded.

'Eighteen.'

'And do you think at eighteen, I'd started courting?'

'I couldn't say, I wasn't there to see you.'

He turned to Joyce again. 'I thought you went to see Sadie Rawlins, what were you doing at Johnson's?'

'Sadie was out,' she snapped back, 'and you have no right to question us like this.'

'All this courting has to stop. I'll see to that,' he added with an air of finality. This giant with aggressive muscle held the hurricane lamp up to my face. 'I'll see her the rest of the way.'

For Joyce's sake I tried to pour oil on troubled waters. 'Well, goodnight Joyce and thanks for your visit.'

'Goodnight,' she replied, 'and thank you for seeing me home.' Suddenly we seemed to have become very formal.

When I got back, Alan and his wife were still up, reading by the oil lamp.

'Back soon, Wilf,' he remarked as I went in.

'Yes, we were waylaid by her stepfather.'

'What!' he said, jumping up off his chair. I related what had happened. 'That's an insult to my house,' he stormed and grabbed his hat, making for the door. His wife grasped him by the arm and countered emotion with reason.

'Now, Alan, leave it till tomorrow when you've calmed down. It's nearly midnight — far too late to go over now,' and so on. In the end her logic prevailed.

Mrs Allen, Joyce's mother, must have heard about it, for she came early next morning in the sulky and apologised for her husband. 'Really,' she told us, 'he's a good father and his bark is worse than his bite,' and went on to say that he'd promised Joyce's grandmother that he would look after her until she was twenty-one. My boss and some of the other settlers, I found out later, held a different opinion. They thought she was too good a source of cheap labour for him to lose, for she had been seen ploughing with a couple of horses as well as milking and doing the housework. Next time we met I asked her how we hadn't seen the light of the lamp before he stepped out from behind the tree. He had it covered under his greatcoat, she explained, but thought she'd seen a flicker of light ahead before we were stopped.

Meetings were now secret trysts. Two friends of mine, Ron, an immigrant who had come out with his father, and Fred Hicks, an Australian lad, wanted me to join in a scheme for waylaying the tyrant and dishing out some punishment for his treatment of Joyce and me. Fred had found out that he was working some land a good distance from the holding and never returned before dark. The idea was to blacken our faces, pounce on him from behind trees and 'beat him up'. Mind, it would have taken three of us, with a big slice of luck thrown in, to have any effect, for the man was forty and one huge ball of aggressive muscle. Really they were heroes to even devise the plan. Despite everything, I wouldn't fall in with it for, after all, Joyce had to live with him and he may have taken it out on her. Even with blackened faces and darkness on our side, he would have guessed who his attackers were, because the three of us spent all our spare time together.

One Saturday, all the settlers went out by truck for a day's outing to the Blackwood River. The weather was perfect and we younger members went into the dark, tree-shaded river for a swim. Brilliant dragonflies hovered over the water, then darted away. Red crested parakeets in the foliage screeched at our intrusion. Snakes slithered into the undergrowth out of harm's way and the whole atmosphere was tinged with mystery. As we entered the water, we wondered what unknown dangers lurked in its depths. The river was sluggish, with leaves of green algae floating on the surface, but when one is young this adds allurement to the experience. Each time we came out of the water, half a dozen leeches had stuck to our bodies. They were black, shiny things and the only way to detach them from the skin was to nip them off by the head. If you tried pulling, they just stretched like elastic without losing their grip. We had a marvellous time swimming, picnicking in the surrounding woods and then lazing in the shade. A break from the hard settlement work was a Godsend.

I had a present for Joyce. It was a powder compact with flowers painted on the outside. The inside was gold-coloured with a mirror on the lid. I wanted an opportunity to give it when the ever-hovering and ominous guardian wasn't around. As the evening approached, Fred Hicks had a suggestion. 'How about taking Joyce and Sadie Rawlins for a walk in the bush?' This idea was pregnant with possibilities but had its drawbacks. It would be a chance to give Joyce her gift, but her father wasn't exactly the man to play ducks and drakes with. I decided to take the bull by the horns for in holiday mood he may have softened. I approached her stepfather with a casual air,

'All right, Mister Alan, if Joyce comes with Sadie for a stroll with Fred and me?'

'Most emphatically not!' he replied. 'After she's twenty one, yes. But not until!'

Ron and Fred thought I was daft for asking, but I was scared that wrath might fall on his stepdaughter. I think Fred had a part in it, but word of it got around and the general reaction was that the parental heavy hand was a bit too weighty. The course of true love was being made a trifle too stormy. At the end of the day, two trucks left to take the settlers to one of their locations where a feast had been prepared. When Joyce and I got into the first truck, along with a dozen or so men with their wives, there was no sign of her father and by the time we got to our destination it was dark. As the truck pulled up at the verandah steps, through the open door oil lamps could be seen hanging from the beams in the big, timbered living room. The two long tables were laden with food and along the centre bottles of Pilsner beer were ranged two deep. Those settlers didn't do anything by halves! The host was a big-boned Indian with an English wife and it was said he could carry two drunken men, one under each arm, away from a bar if they were causing trouble and deposit them outside. One of the settlers, called Sam Oldfield, came up to me as we left the truck.

'Wilf,' he said, 'I believe you have a present for Joyce.'

'Yes,' I replied, 'but I wanted to give it when no one was around in case her father found out.'

'Well, take her into the bush before the other truck arrives and we'll see he doesn't get near.' As we went to climb out of the compound, four of the men including the Indian, moved over to the drop-bars and started idly chatting.

We went a hundred yards or so along the narrow track, barely visible in the darkness, then sat on a convenient log. Joyce was nervous and, to tell the truth, so was I. Have you ever tried to make love, conscious that a human gorilla might pulp you up at any minute? We kissed and then I gave her the powder compact. I don't think she had ever received a present before and the pleasure she showed in receiving it, together with my delight in her pleasure, made us forget everything. Time stood still.The sweet scent of the surrounding forest closed upon us in an emanation of exquisite perfume. The cowslip and the donkey orchid, the wild hyacinth, the crimson honey myrtle and the aromatic eucalyptus all radiated a scent that created a heaven on earth. For a few minutes, we were in a magic land of sweet oblivion. We heard the second truck arrive. Tension mounted again.

'Are you frightened in case he finds out?' I whispered with concern.

'No,' she said, 'he'll, never know. I'll keep it hidden.' We both wondered how the guard was coping so made the best of a last embrace before retracing our steps. When we got back to the rails, the guard was still there.

'Any trouble?' I asked Sam Oldfield. One of the others laughed.

'No. You were all right. When he saw the beer, he forgot everything else!'

There were dances in the schoolroom once a month. They started about nine in the evening and went on till the early hours of the morning. My boss played the fiddle and the old farrier, who was nearly blind, played the concertina with plenty of verve in spite of being wheezy. When they got tired of playing all the known tunes half a dozen times, they used to 'jazz up' hymn tunes. Often we did the quickstep to 'Rock of Ages' and the Lancers to 'Onward Christian Soldiers'. Women were free (I mean got in free) and men paid sixpence. The women brought food in abundance. Eating, drinking, high spirits and dancing continued unflaggingly throughout the night. How we danced the 'light fantastic' with such vigour on top of all the meat pies, cakes, custards, jellies and bottles of beer beats me, but the atmosphere at those dances seemed to be charged with emotion and unbounding energy. We were doing the Lancers at one dance when a tough looking character from our set suddenly dived out of an open window. One or two of us looked around to see if there was any cause for such erratic behaviour — there was! Two bush policemen had appeared at the schoolroom, one at each door. It transpired that there was a maintenance order out against him to support a wife and five children in Perth. It was easy to issue an order. The problem was to catch him.

At the dances I always felt sorry for Joyce. She, with Fred's girl Sadie Rawlins and Ron's girl, would sit together in their dance dresses enjoying every moment, while we three youths clad in our best suits, with razor-edged creases down the front of our trousers (through being under the mattresses since they were last worn) and uncomfortable white collars digging into our necks, hovered around the girls. At eleven o'clock, when we'd had a few dances and refreshments and the revelry was livening up, Joyce would have to go home in the sulky with her mother and stepfather. Even this small concession to her happiness, Mrs Alan told me, was at her mother's insistence that she be allowed a little relaxation.

During the month between the dances, the first fortnight was spent in reminiscences and the next in anticipation, for the women loved the chance to wear their best dresses and, for the men, the beer and the chance of a possible conquest.

A new move

However, I felt restless. The affair with Joyce seemed to be causing as much distress as pleasure and with all the poverty around, the likelihood of saving any money was rather remote. I decided to move to Busselton where the wages were better and the farms more established, with fair sized herds instead of the one or two animals on the local settlements. Through a travelling salesman, I got a job with a Mr and Mrs Peale. He and his wife were Quakers and a better couple never lived. They had married late in life and now owned a herd of pedigree Jersey cows on a good sized farm.

Mr Peale was a big man out from Cumberland and had married an Australian woman. He told me that when he took her to England for a holiday to meet his people, the local villagers were surprised that she was white. When he had written to say that he was married to an Australian woman, they thought she must be an Aborigine (of course, that was in the 1800s). He had been to York College in his youth for a course in agriculture and was an excellent farmer. What he didn't know about farming could have been written on the back of a postage stamp. He always grew the best crops in the neighbourhood and seemed to sail through life with a good natured, easy going self assurance that was reflected in all his work. Sometimes he had me puzzled with the jobs I was given, but the results always proved him right. Once, he had a crop of oats coming on nicely with the stems three or four inches high. 'Wilf,' he said one morning after we'd finished milking. 'After breakfast, I want you to harness two horses to the scarifier and drag it up and down the oat paddock, both ways, and stand on it!' a scarifier is like a metal lattice laid flat with a spike projecting from each intersection. To say the least, I was surprised, but an order is an order, so I just got on with the job. I was just finishing when Alan came over to have a look at it. It looked a sorry mess. 'Now,' he said without batting an eyelid, 'do the same again crossways.'

As I said, orders are orders, so once again I got going. If the crop was completely ruined, that wasn't my fault. The paddock, when finished, was a sight to weep over with churned up bits of stem all over the raked earth, yet the ultimate crop was marvellous with thick, waving grainheads at least four times denser than anyone else's. Later, I asked why he had got me to tear up the crop. 'Well,' he replied, 'from each root stool sprouts one or two stalks, break up the stools and the crop is multiplied accordingly.' So simple for those who know!

Calf love

It was on this farm too that I had the first stirrings of conscience about man's cruelty to farm animals and it happened this way. In the morning I had felled and sawn a jarrah into seven foot billets, ready to split with wedges into fence posts, and was returning after dinner to finish the job. The Australian afternoon was hot and sultry and the cows were standing listlessly in the shade of a copse as I passed on my way back to the bush. The hot, parched earth was alive with a plague of grasshoppers and the sound of myriads of them 'clicking' as they jumped was holding my attention, when suddenly I had a feeling that I was being followed. I looked round and saw that a cow had left the herd and was following about twenty yards behind. It was June. June, a pedigree Jersey, was due for her second calf. I had milked her up to two months previously, when she had been 'dried off' so that nourishment could be provided for the unborn calf. I waited until she caught up, got hold of her horns and turned her around. 'Go on, June,' I said, giving her a slap on the rump, 'back to the herd'. I went on my way again, listening to the grasshoppers and swishing a spray of leaves to keep the troublesome flies away.

After a while, I looked around and saw that June was plodding after me. I repeated the procedure of turning her around in the direction of the now distant herd and tried pushing to give a general idea of what she had to do. It was like trying to move an unwilling mule. A hundred yards further on, I turned to see if she was still following. She was. When I stopped, she stopped. When I moved on again, she did the same. In the end I gave up trying and she followed to where I was working and stood about three yards away, while I got on with the job of log splitting in the shady bush.

After working for an hour or so, I heard a rustling and slight commotion. June had given birth to her calf and was already cleaning around its nose and mouth to let it breathe freely — a function in cattle about which I always marvelled. At four o'clock, it was time to return for milking and the calf, a lemon colour, was already staggering about on uncertain legs after drinking its first milk. I picked it up, body around my neck, legs down the front, and started back for the cowshed. June was obviously delighted. Here was her friend looking after her calf. As she followed at heel, alternately she licked me, then reached up and gave her calf a reassuring lick. I was welcomed as one of the family! Before we had gone far, my shirt became a sticky mess clinging to my back, but I didn't mind. It was June's way of showing affection. On reaching the stockyard, I opened the five-barred gate then walked through and closed it in June's face. She was puzzled but not unduly worried, for wasn't I her friend? In a railed off corner in the back of the cowshed I put some straw down and left the calf in semi-darkness. Immediately it started to bleat plaintively and from outside came a re-assuring 'moo' from its mother. I went back across the stockyard and when the gate was opened, June moved back to let me out, then moved to go in herself, but no — the gate was closed again! Hearing her calf calling, she was now getting really frustrated and distressed, to say the least. Could it possibly be that I wasn't going to let her in? I crossed the small paddock to the house for tea but before going in, I looked back. June had followed me half way, continually 'mooing' in alarm and stood with head raised high as much as to say, 'Haven't you forgotten me?'

That evening, she was driven into the byre with the rest of the herd and milked, but her milk was kept separate for the calf; not from any motive of love that it really belonged to her offspring, but from the fact that it wasn't yet fit for human consumption. Some farmers left cow and calf together for two or three days, but Mr Peale maintained that the sooner the separation, the better. All that night the calling and answering went on continually. I could hear June running around the yard rails, trying to get in. I didn't lose much sleep. I'd heard the same sad routine many times before. Besides, wasn't it generally accepted that they were all just stupid animals?

Next day, when I was coming out of the stockyard, June lowered her head at me in an attitude of charging. I clapped my hands and shooed her away. Poor June — I did feel a pang of remorse — she was desperate. After two or three days of frustrated effort she started to join the herd again, but often disconsolately meandered back to the stockyard, while the occasional 'moo' had now a sad note of resignation. When she calved the next year, she did what some of the other cows did — hid it in the surrounding bush and then rejoined the herd, trying to pretend that nothing had happened, but when they all came milling around at milking time, I knew by her reduced bulk and udder, the dark secret. 'June's had her calf,' I called to Mr Peale as we milked. 'Yes, keep an eye on her when it turns dark,' he called back. After the evening meal, I went out onto the pasture and could dimly see the herd in the distance, silhouetted against the skyline. After waiting a while, I saw the dim shape of one leave the others and make its way into the bush. Thinking she was safe from detection, June was going to feed her calf. I noted roughly the area, because the paddock was so large that, unless you had some idea of where to look, a calf hidden in the surrounding bush could take days to find. Next day, when June was with the herd, I went and stole her calf.

My room was attached to the farmhouse and that night, I had just lit the oil lamp and settled down to read, when I heard a faint 'mooing' in the distance getting louder and louder. It was a cow in distress running towards the stockyard. Yes, it was June. She knew where her calf was. She had learned her second bitter lesson: that I was not only callous, but cunning and treacherous as well.

I never drink milk now. Being a fruitarian, I live on the natural produce of the garden, orchard and field. I leave animals alone to lead their own lives as nature intended. That experience had shown me the evil of separating cow from calf, so that we can steal their milk. We abuse other forms of life and because there are no immediate detrimental effects, we think we have 'got away with it', but the long term results invariably prove the opposite, for the cell structure in cow's milk is too coarse for humans. A survey in America of fits and cot deaths in babies, pinpointed the dairy farming areas as having the highest mortality rate. A human mother's milk is constituted of nourishment needed for a slow growing, active and intellectual child, whereas cow's milk is for the rapid growth of a big-boned, bulky, docile creature. The bovine species also have three stomachs and need mucous forming casein to facilitate the gliding movement of the vegetation they eat. A calf has no such mucous, it leaves a snail-like trail over the grass where it has been eating. This is natural, but the same excess of mucous in a human leads not only to cot deaths but to bronchitis and catarrh in adults. I went to school with the boy from the farm opposite and he used to keep wiping his mouth with a handkerchief to clear away the mucous and spittle when he was speaking.

As I mentioned before, I never drink milk now. No thank you! In return for the love and trust of an animal, I had responded with callousness and treachery. If I do use milk now, it's a soya substitute.

Rivalry

In the local township of Busselton we had the usual dances in the school-room and at one of the dances I fell like a ton of bricks for a girl called Janet Seymour. Janet had come recently out from London and was living with her married sister. She was four years older than me, well educated and what with her brains and beauty combined, I was completely bowled over. Soon, I was going over to her place and escorting her on horseback to the dances, riding my horse Tom. It was about four miles to where she lived, then two miles further to the dance, yet Tom never seemed to tire or object. Counting the return journey, the distances were done twice. He even used to canter quite easily with the two of as astride, which says a lot for his clover and hay diet!

Once, after a bush fire, we had to traverse a narrow track between the trees. It was like riding through a fairy land. The fire had swept along for miles, burning the leaves and undergrowth, but the bark on the trees was still alight and smouldering. Every time a breeze drifted through the forest, the trees glowed red and sparkled like fireworks. The heat was intense but, even bathed in perspiration, we were bewitched by the scene. It was like riding through paradise but with the heat of hell thrown in!

The mention of paradise reminds me of Eden and Eden had a serpent — and so had I in the form of a rival for the favours of my lady love. I loathed him! Quite an unchristian attitude, I'll admit, but still I loathed him. For him, all the signs in the zodiac seemed to be in the ascendant, radiating joy and eventual triumph for his love affairs, whereas mine were in a descending spiral, destined to end in despair and ultimate failure. For one thing, he was a wizard at cricket and to be a good cricket player in Australia gives a person status regardless! It was said as a joke but with a strong element of truth, that the first question asked of a stranger applying for a job was, 'Can you play cricket?' If he could and proved it on the pitch, then a steady job was assured. Even if one farmer ran out of work for him, he'd be engaged by another within the community.

Every Sunday, the local community used to congregate to watch a cricket match and this rival of mine was in great demand. Fielding at slip, he would stand half bent and dopey looking, but never did a ball get past him. He could shoot out an arm and catch a ball with the speed and deadly accuracy of a striking rattlesnake. As for me, I was a real butterfingers and couldn't catch a ball to save my life. His efforts were always met with a cheer, mine with a groan. Besides, he owned a good sized farm that his parents had bought him. So what with one thing and another, he was well established and all that was missing was a love-bird. My total assets were a knock kneed hack and the wherewithal to produce a brood.

Janet's brother-in-law, Bert, probably sensing the rivalry and my reluctance to getting tied up, tried to press the issue. He told me about a deserted smallholding lying waste. 'Why not pop the question,' he suggested, 'and settle in there? It's close to my place and Ellen and Janet could visit one another.' I told him that I'd seen the place and that the surrounding undergrowth was alive with snakes and I wanted to save more money first. How would we live until we had a few cows and poultry? 'But with help form Ellen and me, you could get started,' he countered to my evasions. But the idea of married life had me really scared. To tie myself to a life of bondage with anyone seemed too final and fatal to me. The subconscious fear of marriage ruled. I cooled the romance off by not seeing her so often. We started having 'words'. I hadn't gone to the last dance. Why hadn't I sent word by the milk lorry driver or ridden over to give a reason? What happened last Sunday?

In the end the inevitable happened. Mr Jolly, the lorry driver who also collected and delivered the mail, brought a letter from Janet that stated that our affair had ended. Immediately I was plunged into a depression of grief and self-pity, followed by a fit of jealous temper — such is the unreasoning logic of youth! I replied by saying she was unfaithful, perfidious and all manner of things; unwittingly proving that love and hate are truly closely linked. I enclosed a handkerchief that I knew she had laboriously hemstitched for a present. Then after I'd sent the letter, reaction set in. I was overcome with remorse for having written it! Night after sleepless night I tossed and turned in bed, imagining her in the arms of that odious cricket fanatic. In the end I hit on a plan. I would ride over and try to fix up the romance again.

One bright moonlit night I waited until everything was quiet and everyone asleep. Then I made my way stealthily to the stockyard where I'd left Tom in readiness. As I saddled him up, the only sound was an occasional bark from a dingo in the distance. The bright moonlight was perfect for the mission in hand and my spirits, which had been at a low ebb of despair since the letter had arrived, suddenly rocketed with the thought of seeing my true love again. Tom might yet again be the willing charger carrying a double load. The drive from the stockyard to the bush track was stony and passed close to the house. I wanted this delicate mission to be secret. I led Tom by the reins slowly. Every time his metal shoes clinked on a stone, I stopped, waited a while then moved on again. I stopped so often that in the end Tom seemed to sense that silence was called for. At the slightest clink of metal he would stop and look at me with ears pricked forward, as much as to say, 'I've done it again!' Once on the sandy bush track, we were off at a fast canter and away on our journey with the prospect that alternately filled me with hope and foreboding. When passing settlers' bungalows, I made a detour into the bush to escape detection. As I approached one farm, a horse in the stable whinnied and mine answered. I stopped, hidden by the trees, and prayed that Tom would remain quiet. The settler came out with a hurricane lamp, had a cursory look inside the stable, then went in again. I went on and finally arrived at the final place of decision. Now you may be wondering why I went on this mission at night and not in broad daylight like any other self-respecting wooer, but I had my reasons. You see, Janet's sister Ellen, being married and therefore more practical, favoured my rival, so I wanted Janet on her own.

I dismounted about a hundred yards from the house, slipped the horse's reins over a handy tree branch, then quietly proceeded on foot. Now if you've never broken into a house, unsure of your reception when discovered and equally unsure of the ultimate outcome, then you've missed one of the highlights of life! Doors in buildings in the bush were never locked, so there was no obstacle there. The danger of detection lay in the creaking veranda boards and the two doors that had to be opened; one into the house and the other into her bedroom. One or two of the boards creaked ominously under my stealthy tread. I stood for a while listening — but all remained silent. Each creak of a hinge froze me to the spot as inch by inch I opened each door.

At long last, I stood in her bedroom. The moon was now covered by cloud. I stood in the darkness hesitant and deliberating my next move. If the moon came out or I touched her, even gently, would she scream, thinking it was a stranger? I stood still unsure of my next move, when a calm voice in the darkness whispered, 'Is that you Wilf?'

I went quietly over and sat on her bed. 'How did you know it was me?' I whispered.

'I've been expecting you!' she replied. I took her hand in mine and realised the worst. She was wearing an engagement ring.

'Billy?' I whispered. She nodded slowly, then took her hands away. When she placed them in mine again, the ring was missing.

I left about four in the morning. Work started at six, getting the cows rounded up for milking. A fitful moon played hide and seek with the clouds when I mounted Tom again. To save time, I risked a short cut through the bush, but usually I've found that so-called short cuts are fatal unless one is sure of the way, and it proved no exception on this occasion. Soon I came to a fork in the track and didn't know which one to take. In the darkness, both tracks looked alike. There was no way of telling which one had been recently used. I gave the horse free rein, relying on his homing instinct. He took the track leading to the left. A couple of hundred yards further on the moon appeared from behind the clouds, just in time for me to see a thick tree branch sticking out at right angles across the track. I ducked quickly and went on.

Eventually I came to a circular, sleeper-cutters' clearing. These clearings were left by the Italians who, working in gangs, would find a batch of straight jarrahs, fell them and cut them into sleepers, then move on again. In the fitful moonlight I looked for a way out on the far side. The clearing was so desolate and quiet in the pre-dawn stillness that one had the impression that life did not exist. A place where people had lived and left has always a peculiar melancholy, unlike that of untrammelled ground. There was no other way out, so after circling the clearing, I set Tom off at a canter back up the track we had come down. I was getting worried about time too, as dawn was approaching. The other track must be the right one, I was musing as I cantered along, when suddenly — wallop! — I was hit in the face with such force that I was knocked clean out of the saddle and found myself dangling upside down with both feet still in the stirrups. I'd clean forgotten about the overhanging branch! Tom started rearing and circling around, snorting with fright. 'Whey, Tom. Whoa, Tom. Steady, Tom. Whoa, Boy,' I kept saying to him, trying to impart a calmness I was far from feeling myself, while I tried to wriggle free the foot that was higher than the other. If he had bolted, it would have been death for me. Eventually, after many

'Wheys and Whoas', I managed to free one foot, then hopped around and jumped back into the saddle.

At the fork, I took the other track. Daylight had arrived when I got back. Tom was unsaddled and released into the paddock before I went into my room to change into my work clothes. I'd noticed that the cows were already milling around the byres, so time was on my side. When I went over to the milking shed, Mr Peale was already there, leading in the cows.

'Morning, Wilf,' he called out as I approached.

'Morning, Mr Peale,' I answered, stifling a yawn and trying to look as if I'd just got out of bed. But he wasn't listening. He just stared at me dumb-founded.

'What's happened?' he gasped.

'Nothing,' I replied, feeling guilty, but trying to look the picture of innocence.

'Go back to the house,' he said, looking as though he was seeing a ghost, 'and take a look at your face in the mirror.'

I did and got a shock. It was covered with dried blood. The branch that knocked me off the horse had scraped up my face and taken the skin with it, but in the excitement of the moment and with death staring me in the face, I hadn't even noticed, nor felt any pain. I washed the blood off with cold water, dabbed it fairly dry, then went back to the milking.

When we went back to the house, Mrs Peale was preparing breakfast but stopped operations while she stared at my face. 'What's happened?'

I explained that I had tripped up and fallen against a veranda post.

'But both your eyes are black!' she added incredulously. When she left the room to get some bandage, Mr Peale smiled suddenly and asked quietly, 'Have a fight with a rival last night?' I gave a sickly, gory grin in reply. He may have heard Tom and I going or returning from our night mission. He guessed that questions were not welcome and didn't say any more.

Working with horses

Dan was a Clydesdale horse. He was wall-eyed and could be mischievous, but apart from this he was quite reliable. Clearing the bush for conversion into grassland entailed sapping the large redgums and jarrahs, felling the smaller ones, then six months later, when the sap has dried out, setting it alight after encircling the area with a fire break. Most of the scrub and small trees get burnt, but the larger trunks and logs must be dragged alongside one another and fired again. Dan used to be harnessed up in the 'spider' for the work. The spider consisted of two chains leading from the hames, supported by a leather back-strap, passing around a wooden space-bar behind the rear legs and terminating in a single chain with a large hook at the end. This was used to drag the logs together and an obedient horse is necessary to start and stop immediately upon the order. Dan and I worked in perfect harmony.

One of the tasks was to roll trunks onto the top of others and this entailed dragging one alongside, wrapping the chain round the trunk, so that when the horse pulled, it rolled up and onto the top. This is where a good horse proves his worth. If he stops too soon, the trunk rolls back; if too late, it rolls right over and down the other side. I could work this to a nicety with Dan. When everything was ready I would shout, 'Go on Dan!' He would take a short run to get the trunk rolling up, then 'Whey!' and he would stop dead, with ears back, waiting for the next order. If it wasn't far enough, I would shout, 'A bit, Dan — Whey!' I could get him to juggle them exactly into place.

One area we were clearing was fairly close to the farmhouse and at eleven in the morning Mrs Peale used to ring a bell for morning break. Animals have a marvellous sense of time and as eleven o'clock was getting near, Dan had one ear turned back, listening to me, and the other pricked forward listening for the bell. If the chain was loose when the bell rang, he was off and all my shouts for him to wait fell on deaf ears. He looked the picture of guilt as he trundled away, but it was break-time and he wanted his nose-bag of chaff. I knew precisely what he was thinking. 'If I was daft enough to work after the bell had gone, that was up to me!'

Another time, when we were snigging, I pulled him by the bridle towards me. Now when a horse moves sideways, it always takes long strides with the forelegs. This particular time he took a longer stride than usual and his massive hoof landed on top of my foot. Luckily, I had heavy boots on and the ground gave a bit, but I was trapped. 'Go over, Dan,' I shouted but he wouldn't move — just stood with forelegs splayed out like the statue of a ballet-dancing dray horse.

Here I must digress a little and let you into a secret. You see, Dan, as big as he was, had had no schooling. He didn't even know his ABC. So if Dan was in any unusual situation and knew I wanted him to do something, but wasn't sure what I meant, he just stood awkwardly and motionless, not because he didn't want to comply, but in case he made the wrong move. This was one of those occasions. I pushed his head away, hoping his hoof would follow, but it didn't. 'Dan!' I shouted, 'your hoof, it's on my foot!' I pleaded and begged, then in desperation hit him on the side of the face. He moved it sideways out of reach and looked the picture of bashfulness. I bent down, grasped the long hair on his fetlock and heaved. He did not respond. The only thing I could do was wait. After a while he got the idea we were resting, so took the weight off one hind leg and tipped the hoof up, gave a sigh of contentment, and that was that. In the sweltering Australian sun, man and beast presented a tableau of the stillness of eternity. After resting that leg, he gave another sigh and reversed the order; heaved his rump over from north to south and tipped the other hoof up. My chief concern was to make sure he didn't move over towards me. For if he put all his weight on my foot, the bones would have snapped like matchsticks. After what seemed an eternity, he lifted the hoof off my foot and, praise the Lord, I was free!

When I took the rein and limped on again, Dan gave his usual sigh of resignation and lumbered on alongside. He hadn't had a clue what all the fuss had been about.

Animals have always struck me as being fundamentally very similar to humans. The only barrier being their lack of speech (which, come to think of it, might be an advantage if we possessed the same deficiency at times). There is an understanding which springs up between man and animal much the same as man to man, for after I had, as you might say, 'seen the light', I was appalled by a feeling of revulsion to think that I had been so depraved as to kill animals for food. If people who eat one another are cannibals, then animal eaters are, it seems to me, claimants to the same appellation.

Once after dinner, as Dan was being harnessed up at the saddle room door, the heat was overpowering. The sun shone down pitilessly from a cloudless sky. I put on his bridle and collar, then went in again for the hames. On coming out again, I saw that Dan was off, lumbering back towards the clearing like a pet elephant. 'Come back, you fathead,' I shouted after him, 'you haven't the hames on yet!' He stopped, gave such a sigh, then turned around and trundled back, as much as to say, 'Hurry up! This heat is killing me!' It was really funny. I don't think he was able to fathom out what I said. It was probably mental telepathy.

Dan and I used to go muck-spreading and doing various jobs on the farm that called for cart work and Dan, being mischievous, always liked his little game at dinner time. I would drive the cart into the compound, then swing around and back him up into the byres. When the back of the cart was within a yard or so of the building, I'd shout 'Whey, Dan, Whoa!' But Dan would neither Whey nor Whoa. He would keep on backing until he heard the cart bang into the byres and, with his strength, the effect on the wooden building was shattering, to say the least. Once, I got so exasperated at his cussedness that I made him back over and over again until in the end, he gave in and stopped when he was told. I got off the cart, removed the snaffle, put on his nosebag of oats and chaff, then went over to the farm for dinner. I was feeling really pleased that I had won the battle of wits and, before going indoors, looked to see if he was all right. He was munching his oats and with his head raised and ears pricked forward was looking across at me. As soon as he saw me looking, he deliberately backed the cart into the byres with a resounding crash, as much as to say, 'Who's won now?'

Oh, yes! Dan could be mischievous, but like all herbivorous animals, he was never aggressive. He would never bite or kick or wilfully hurt anyone. If I had occasion to raise his hind leg because it was caught in the traces, he would lower it very slowly, making sure everything was clear. One tip I got from an Australian horsewoman, was never to grasp or touch a horse's hind leg suddenly. Always run your hand down from the flank; otherwise it kicks out in a reflex action. It may be hard to believe but a cow has a more dangerous kick than a horse. A horse kicks straight back, but a cow lifts her hind leg and kicks outward and back, which is a lesson you learn at your cost if she is being milked.

Of course, even in animals, you will find the exception that breaks the rules; such as the dish-faced or wall-eyed horse but usually, if a horse bites and kicks, it is because of ill-treatment and uses those tactics as its means of self-defence. However, there is no doubt in my mind, after many experiences and close contact with animals, that far from being insensitive brutes, as they are often labelled, they are far more sensitive than many humans and have a gift of discernment and insight seldom found in humans. An animal picks up radiations and knows the real you. There is no hoodwinking them. They know. Of course I'm referring to the herbivores that don't lust for a kill. In fact, unwittingly they practise more Christian ideals than many humans do, and until man adopts these same qualities by embracing all life as one, so will he continue to wallow in the mire of disease and insanity that still holds him down. The original state of harmony should be everywhere and the best way to return to Utopia is to stop killing and abusing other forms of life. For where is the philosopher or saint who can couple this depravity with harmony?

Settlers and Aborigines

Joe Shapcott and I met up again in Busselton about this time. Joe had worked on one of the settlements and used to come up to the schoolroom dances where my boss had jazzed up the hymn tunes on his fiddle. He was the tall, athletic type and turned out to be a good and faithful friend. He was going up to Perth for a week's holiday and then travelling on North to the wheat belt. He was keen to get a bush-clearing contract and asked me to join him. The lure of travel and fresh experience prevailed, so after a reluctant farewell to Mr and Mrs Peale, we took the train to Perth and settled in at the Salvation Army Hostel: one shilling a night bed and breakfast. After the week's holiday, we went to the labour exchange every day and soon obtained a job offered to clear twenty acres of land for a Miss Simms way up in the wheat country. We were loath to leave the hostel and the 'Salvation lasses' with whom we got on so well during our short stay, but funds were already running low and 'needs must, when the devil drives', so we travelled light and 'jumped the rattler' to our destination.

Miss Simms turned out to be a woman in her eighties, a second generation Australian and as hard a nut to crack as the toughest ranger. Her father had been speared by an Aborigine over a dispute about rations. He had worked them together, regardless of their clan or groups; a fatal mistake often made in early days because of ignorance. For men and women of different groups to work, eat or even sit together was, to them, absolutely taboo and many an early settler was killed and probably didn't know the reason. They mixed only when courting and a young man or woman knew from which group to select a mate. If they broke this law, the fleeing couple were hunted down and killed. Only the Aborigines knew the intricacies of the system. I asked one or two old Australians how the group system worked and even they admitted they couldn't fathom it out. The only solution they could guess at was that it prevented in-breeding.

Aborigines are marvellous trackers too. They can follow at a jog trot the track made by a man through the bush, following the trail by smell and marks in the undergrowth and foliage. Not only are they good at tracking but have a deep insight into human reactions. There was a police case of a man who had become mental and disappeared into the bush. Their Aborigine tracker was put on his trail. He trotted along until eventually he came to a river where the man was found splashing about in the water. The police were going to go straight in. 'No, leave him to me,' cautioned the Aborigine. 'You run in this side. He run out the other side.' He went in the river, splashing and playing about but getting nearer and nearer the patient until eventually they were holding hands and they continued to play until they were back to the bank.

Alan Peale told me that when he was managing a sheep station, they had an Aborigine girl called Rosie working in the house. One morning she came in in high glee and doubled up in laughter about the white sheep shearers. They had seen what they took to be the track of a snake in the sandy soil and, armed with sticks, were following it up, for in Australia the unwritten law is that when you see a snake you kill it, because it may be the death of someone some day. (Very few of the snakes are poisonous. The belief probably springs from the universal fear of them). Anyway Rosie, the Aborigine girl, was highly amused and could hardly speak for laughing. 'It's no snake they follow. It ruptured ram!' They were so good at tracking that if half a dozen horses were in a paddock and one broke loose, they could tell by the hoof marks which one it was. The Aborigines were no fools and were quick to learn western ways. They had, of course, one or two faults. Rosie, for instance, was good at housework but didn't like to have a bath. For no apparent reason she would disappear suddenly for about six weeks, then reappear and start working again as if nothing unusual had happened. When asked where she had been, she would say casually, 'To a corroboree.' This was a periodical gathering of the aborigines for a social get-together that went on for weeks with nocturnal dancing and festivities. Probably this was a time for partner picking as well, but nothing could stop their disappearance at such times. They also had the unsocial habit of rubbing their bodies with fat from the iguana. Now the ground is alive with ants and ants abhor grease and oil, so an Aborigine can sit anywhere with impunity and never an ant will go near him. The drawback is that in a house, the pong of stale iguana fat will keep more than the ants away and one of the hardest lessons was to teach an Aborigine to wash or have a bath!

To return to Miss Simms. We looked over the land to be cleared. Most of the trees were dead and had fallen. There were no axe marks in the wood. Probably they had been ringmarked earlier, for the gaunt bare trunks glistened in the bright sunlight. We would need to buy gelignite and detonators for splitting the wood and the clearing would be awkward to work, for it was a steep hillside with rock outcroppings. We decided on a price of four pounds an acre — eighty pounds the lot. We went back to her bungalow. It had a wide veranda at the front, on which we invariably found her rocking gently to and fro on an old Victorian rocking chair. Also she had a middle-aged woman housekeeper. Joe left it to me to negotiate.

'Well, Miss Simms,' I said, after the usual formalities, 'we've decided on a price of four pounds an acre to clear your land.'

She remained silent, rocking gently in the chair, then poured more whisky into the glass by her side. She leant back and started rocking again. 'Two pounds or the contract's off, boys,' she said with an air of finality.

'Remember,' I countered, 'we'll have to buy explosives out of the money and working on that steep hillside won't be easy.'

'Yes, but the trees are mostly fallen or dead — a match and they'll burn themselves!'

'All right,' I countered again, 'three pounds an acre — and you buy the explosives.'

She wasn't to be moved. 'Forty pounds the lot, boys.' You buy the explosives and the contract's yours.' She rocked harder in the chair, awaiting our decision.

I looked at Joe. We were rock bottom in funds and knew that work wasn't easy to come by. He nodded. 'Right,' I replied, 'it's settled.'

Her attitude took a complete somersault. From being tight-lipped and unyielding, she became most hospitable and friendly. 'Joan!' she called, 'bring out two more glasses and another bottle of whisky, this one's nearly empty.' The housekeeper brought onto the veranda, the bottle of whisky, two tumblers and a small jug of water on a tray. 'The doctor's ordered me to take whisky for my heart, but I have to pay for it,' she informed us as the tray was deposited on her small side table. We spent quite an enjoyable hour with her, talking about England, which she obviously loved to hear about. She told us about her father and how he was speared while giving out rations to his aborigine workers. Later, after having our fair share of whisky, we left to set up camp.

The burning, as we predicted, proved to be no simple task and being on a steep hillside added frustration to the work. In theory it should have been easy to roll a higher trunk to join up with a lower one for burning, but it didn't work out that way in practice. Once a trunk started to roll, it was a matter of conjecture which course it would take and when it would stop — if ever. It gained speed at an alarming rate, bouncing and twisting and either missed, or ended up at right angles to the other. Then would start the laborious job of crow-barring it into place. Many a time one of us would hear a shout from higher up the hill. 'Watch out!' and looking up, see a huge trunk with jagged, stumpy remains of branches at one end, bounding down bent on the destruction of life and limb. The danger was that their course was so erratic, you didn't know which way to jump. Joe once ran the wrong way and took a lucky flying leap over a monster as it thundered past in a cloud of dust. The trees trapped by boulders were split open by charges of explosives, for solid wood won't burn on its own. The parcel of land took a month to clear. Even then there was a huge girthed but short trunk left on the plateau at the top. We decided to leave it because we had used up all the gelignite and to buy more was out of the question. Besides, it couldn't be seen from her bungalow. So we called it a day.

After breakfast next morning, Joe and I got spruced up and went for our money, for we were badly in need of it. We owed the storekeeper at the siding nearly ten pounds for rations and explosives. We had got a lift from a passing truck into the siding after fixing up the contract and asked him for rations on credit. He was a typical colonial, free and easy, with a generous nature.

'Who're you going to work for?' he asked.

'Miss Simms — clearing twenty acres.'

'Right. Tell me what you want and I'll take you back with the rations in the car.' He even called twice to make sure we weren't running short. It was a case of a friend in need, a friend indeed.

He supplied all the explosives as well.

When we arrived, Miss Simms was, as usual, sitting in her rocking chair. 'Good Morning, Miss Simms,' I called as I approached the veranda steps, 'the contract's finished.'

She took not the slightest notice as Joe and I sat on the veranda steps.

'Warm morning again,' I remarked, as Joe and I casually whisked flies away from our heads. Her fast, short rocking did not bode well for us.

'You're getting no cheque yet!' she suddenly barked out, 'not until I've gone over the ground and seen your work.' We took this as stalling for time and a reluctance to part with cash. For to consider that a woman in her eighties would climb that veritable mountain was just laughable.

'But you'll never climb that hill,' said Joe incredulously.

'Oh, yes I will,' she snapped back. 'I'll have a look at it tomorrow. Call in the evening.'

We played up to her whims. 'All right, Miss Simms. We'll call again.'

On the way back to the camp, Joe got a bit worried.

'She couldn't possibly climb to the top and see the trunk?' he mused as we went along.

'No, not a chance,' I reassured him, 'nearly ninety and a weak heart — never!'

We called again the next midday, expecting to find her as usual in the rocking chair — but she wasn't! The housekeeper came out.

'Miss Simms in?'

'No. She's gone out to look at your work.' We couldn't believe it and must have looked incredulous. 'Oh yes, she's gone all right,' she continued. 'She left just after six this morning with a flask of whisky and some sandwiches.'

We must still have looked incredulous. Not only was the hill steep but there were outcroppings of boulders to climb over. The housekeeper went inside again and came out with binoculars. She scanned the hill opposite, finally focusing on a point halfway up.

'Yes, there she is,' she assured us as she adjusted the lenses,'I think she's having a meal now.' We took the binoculars in turn and sure enough, there she was, a diminutive figure about half a mile away sitting on the hillside. When I looked, she was having a swig of whisky.

Her steers had been moved by drovers onto pasture land near the sea during the hot dry summer months. The land we had cleared was to add to her winter pasturage. The trunk at the top that couln't be burned would in no way affect the growing area, but she might use it as a lever to dodge paying. I got a bit worried. So was Joe. Could the peppery, whisky-swiggin' invalid possibly reach the top? Surely not. She would probably eat her lunch and return. The housekeeper advised us to come back the following afternoon to give her a chance to recuperate after the long excursion.

We returned at about four o'clock the next day. She was back in the rocking chair and judging by the speed of the rocks, the omens were not good!

'Everything all right, Miss Simms?' I asked in a breezy manner. She didn't answer, just rocked harder. 'Satisfied with the work?'

She stopped rocking, took a nip of whisky, then started rocking again. 'No I am not and you're getting no money out of me!'

'But a contract's a contract and has to be paid.'

'You're a couple of rogues!' she snapped back.

'How can we be rogues? We've cleared your land.'

'I thought you were rogues when I first set eyes on you and now I know!' Both Joe and I were getting a bit nettled by her attitude. Was she going to swing a quick one on us and refuse to pay? We guessed she had seen the big-girthed, short trunk that was left, but if she was going to use that as an excuse for not paying, it would be sharp practice on her part.

'Give a reason for your attitude,' I asked.

'You both know nicely the reason. There's a big lump of timber left on that hilltop and until that's burnt off you're getting no cheque off me.'

Joe spoke up. He was a miner's son, a good worker, who could keep a steady pace for hours. Subsequently I did quite a lot of clearing with Joe. Always we worked in half-chain widths and in the mornings I would forge ahead of Joe's pace, but later in the day he would draw level with me and extend his width to counter my flagging energies. The only thing I had against Joe was on a point of hygiene, for he would persist in washing his feet in our outsize frying pan. 'Timber or no timber,' he said sharply, 'you've had a good bargain. Forty pound for clearing all those acres and we aren't paying out any more for explosives.'

I added to Joe's remarks by explaining the difficulty of burning the lone piece of timber without any surrounding smaller wood to get it going. She started rocking more slowly as we explained our situation without resorting to buying more gelignite and detonators. Suddenly her mood did a complete somersault again. 'Come in boys and get your cheque!' So saying, she got off the chair and led us into a dismal Victorian drawing room. It took a while for our eyes to discern the contents after the brilliant sunshine outside. Thick, faded velvet curtains hung at the window, a cushioned settee and wickerwork easy chairs were arranged around the room. A grandfather clock stood in one corner laboriously ticking out eternity and in the centre of the room stood a table covered with a thick, tasselled, maroon cloth. It gave the feeling of stepping back a hundred years in time.

'Joan,' she called, 'bring the whisky and cheque book.'

We sat on high backed seats at each side of the table and when Joan brought in the whisky we were told to help ourselves. Joe poured himself half a tumbler of the spirit. I let manners overcome desire and only took a quarter, filling up with water. She took a quarter too, but sipped it neat. She passed the cheque book across the table. 'Make out your own cheque boys.' This move surprised us, as she was obviously reluctant to part with cash. It didn't fit in. I dated a blank cheque and made it out: 'Pay the bearer the sum of forty pounds,' then passed it back over the table for her to sign. She took another sip of whisky, dipped her pen in the ink and bent over it. She sat motionless, looking at the cheque. Joe rolled himself a cigarette. I sipped some more whisky. The heat in the room was stifling. Not a breath of air moved. One or two blow flies droned around. Apart from them and the clock, the silence, the gloom and the heat were oppressive. She still sat like a statue, with head bent down. Joe and I looked at each other, wondering what was wrong and starting to feel a bit embarrassed. My voice shattered the silence.

'Everything all right, Miss Simms?'

She didn't answer and we suddenly realised that she was weeping. We were now most embarrassed. I rolled myself a fag and Joe had another drink, then broke the silence again.

'Feeling all right ,Miss Simms?' he asked in a conciliatory tone. She tried to dry her eyes.

'It's this beautiful writing,' she sobbed. 'I cannot write,' and again she wept copiously. 'With all my cattle, land and money — I was never educated — I cannot write,' and she wept again in silence. We felt really sorry for her, but all the same, wished she would sign the cheque. After this, the conversation became more balanced and less emotional. She plied us both with more drink, while she asked questions about England, her favourite topic, and after a long time, passed the cheque across the table to me. I tried to look casual as I scanned the signature, but my eyes nearly popped out of my head. I slid it over to Joe. He looked, then quickly looked again. He was obviously shaken too, for, where the signature should have been, were three shaky crosses! We were both thinking the same; would it be cashed?

We left as soon as possible and although it was getting late in the day, we got a lift into the siding on a passing lorry and made straight for the saloon. A big-boned Australian climbed the veranda steps in front of us. Half a dozen men lounged against the rails. He called out to them as he got to the swing doors, 'If there's any bastard here, he can have a drink.' They all followed him in. We pushed our way through the crowd at the bar.

'Two Pilsners,' said Joe, slamming the cheque on the counter. The publican casually looked at it, brought over two bottles and glasses, picked up the cheque and took a wad of notes from an old, high cash register. When he had paid the money over, I remarked, 'Those three crosses O.K. then?'

'Sure,' he drawled, 'I'd know Miss Simms' three crosses anywhere. That cheque could have three more noughts and still be cashed.'

While in the saloon, we decided to try our luck up in the goldfields, for after paying the storekeeper, we would still have thirty pounds in credit. Next day, before leaving we went over to see Miss Simms. Her nephew had just arrived to drive her back to the coast station. She wanted us to return with her to the coast and work for her there, but we didn't fancy it. She was a bit too tight with the cash. In fact, her nephew came back to the camp with us for a chat and even he thought we were wise not to go.

'I've had to come over,' he said, 'because she cannot even keep a chauffeur more than a month.' Besides, I've always preferred men employers. A woman, as an employer, isn't balanced and just considers her own interests, regardless of fairness to the employee. Neither is it natural for a woman to hold power over men. Throughout nature the male is dominant and the leader and for women to be dictating to men is as illogical as children dictating to women.

The goldfields

We packed our kit and made for Coolgardie. Coolgardie was the first place where gold was struck in the last century. It was truly a deserted city when we arrived, for the gold had soon petered out and everyone had moved twenty miles further on, to a place called Kalgoordie, where a much richer field had been found. Empty houses, with doors swinging and banging in the wind, were yours for the taking and in the main street empty shops, banks, saloons and a lone cinema stood like ghosts of the departed. Sandy dust covered everything and the whole aspect was one of death and gloom. We looked in one bank with a palatial front and, lying stretched out on the polished counter, was a swaggie, with his boots under his head for a pillow. The only place occupied was a nunnery and we heard later that the nuns never turned away a 'down and out', without giving him a meal for a little work. Anyway, there was nothing to be gained from hanging around, so we went to the siding to await the trains passing through and when a slow moving train came along we 'jumped it'.

Kalgoorlie turned out to be as busy and thriving as Coolgardie had been deserted and derelict. It was a town set on a barren, wind-swept plain. Tramcars ran from the desert edge through the town, then turned around when they came to the desert again. It was a town set in the middle of nowhere! Joe and I headed for the museum to find out, with the rosy optimism of youth, what gold-bearing rocks looked like, so that we would recognise our bonanza when we struck it. It turned out to be the nearest we got to the stuff.

We dug our own 'tinpot' mine on the edge of the town and for days, we dug, and dug, and dug. We found green-spotted, blue, red, grey, brown and black-spotted but not a single yellow-spotted stone. One of us dug while the other brought the buckets of sticky, sandy gravel to the suface. In next to no time, our mine looked like the excavations to a Pharaoh's tomb. It sloped down for some six feet and then the facing wall was cut away to make, or break, our fortune. On this work one can get the 'gold bug' which is exactly similar to gambling; expecting your next selection to be a winner. For you never know what the next shovelful is going to reveal. It might be a gold nugget worth thousands or, on the other hand, it might not, but you keep on going on and on, in hope. Some of the other men were re-blowing the sand brought up from the old mines. They had a contraption called a 'hopper'. A narrow based container is filled with sand and as it falls through the small opening, a foot pedal works a bellows that blows the sand and dust away, but the gold dust, being heavier, falls onto a metal plate.

Most of the men work for about six months, then get the gold dust cashed by the bank. Then they 'live it up' for a week or two before returning to the treadmill for another stint. Most of the men are loners. Joe and I soon found it was a waste of time trying to be friendly. If we called out a friendly word as we passed, they just ignored it or at best simply grunted in reply. They didn't even speak to each other, never mind to strangers. We decided that they thought everyone was interested solely in trying to pinch their gold dust. A more unfriendly, taciturn lot it would be hard to find.

After a month of hard and unrewarding work, we decided to quit. Our cash was running out and if we kept on digging in the tomb, the spectre of madness or death from a cave-in would soon loom up. Besides, we had not even unearthed a rusty tin can let alone a nugget of gold. So we called it a day. We went round the big mines trying to get a job. They were like coal mines in England with shifts of men going down in cages. We tried the 'Alice' mine, the 'Lucky Strike' and the 'Aunt Sally' but drew a blank. Jobs were at a premium. Most of the miners we saw were Italians and we heard that periodically there would be a flare up, when Australians would rebel against the foreign labour and burn all their shanties down. It had, at times, even got so bad that both sides dug trenches and used firearms; but after being cleared out, the Italians wormed their way back and this led to another flare-up. The main reason why they were disliked was their habit of undercutting wages in order to get work in the mines. Joe and I had wondered how rows of shacks came to be burned to the ground. Now we knew!

Stan Laker, an Australian I knew, had worked in one of the mines but got the sack when he tried a 'get rich quick' stunt that didn't come off! Before I tell you how it happened, I must explain the rules concerning stealing that are peculiar to gold mines. There are illegal buyers in a few of the shacks and if a miner gets to one of these without being caught, then no questions are asked. In making a shady deal, the miner receives a poor price for his ill-gotten gold and runs the risk of losing his job and a possible prosecution. A miner arriving for work must strip in one room and put on his mine working clothes in another. On finishing work the process is reversed. He takes off his work clothes and walks naked into the other room. All this is done under the scrutiny of two detectives, who stand at the intervening door watching for anything suspicious.

Gold in the mines is not in handy lumps, it is within the rock and for a man to pinch a lump of that, he would have to stagger out like Atlas supporting the world, but at times small chips of gold are found and these are what the men contrive to steal. Stan found one such piece, the size of a pea, and before going to the surface, he rolled it with some chewing gum into the hairs of his armpit. The detectives did not even seem suspicious when he walked through the short passage to change into his outdoor clothes, but the armpit is not exactly the toughest part of the body and the bit of gold started scratching. He noticed one of the 'tecs seemed to get uncomfortably interested as he moved towards the outer door. He called out, 'Stand where you are, Laker!' Stan pretended not to hear and walked out through the door. Both 'tecs called and started to go after him. Stan immediately took to his heels with them in full chase. As he ran, he disentangled the bit of gold and, running behind an airshaft, threw it in. Of course they found nothing when he was taken back and searched and he denied any intent to steal, but next morning, before going to the cage, he was called into the office, paid up to date and sacked. Some used to swallow their booty and await the course of nature.

The gold-bearing rock is sent from the mines to government crushers. I knew a Mr Wright who had managed a government crushing plant and he told me that payment for the service was the gold dust washed from the crushers each evening.

Return to Perth

Joe suggested that we return to Perth. He had migrated under a Salvation Army scheme and he was sure they would find us a job. Another point in favour of this suggestion was the prospect of meeting up with the Army lasses again. So Joe put forward that suggestion which was seconded by me and carried by both.

As we were nearly broke again, we decided to travel down to Perth at the government's expense on the state railway: in other words 'jump the rattler'. The best time to jump into a goods train was while it was at a siding, hissing and steaming as it filled up with water from the overhead tanks. The method was to undo a corner of a tarpaulin under cover of darkness, clamber into the truck, then leave the rest to St. Christopher. The swaggies on those trains could be counted by the dozen. Sometimes we jumped down into a high sided truck in the dark and were greeted with a volley of oaths. We had landed on one of our own fraternity lying flat against the side. Sometimes, at a siding down the line, the guard would come along the train and clear out all the human flotsam. He could tell where we were by the flapping tarpaulins, but this didn't particularly worry us or, for that matter anyone else, for we simply sat around near the track waiting for it to move again or for the next train to come along. The guards were obviously complying with routine orders, for sometimes they would tell us the waggons were going to be unloaded and the time of the next train! Of course, unemployment was rife in those years and Australians have great sympathy for anyone down on their luck.

At one station we were evicted. It was turned midnight and raining, so Joe and I decided to look for shelter and kip down for the night. In the darkness we could discern the outlines of some shacks about a hundred yards away. We made our way towards them and eventually found what appeared to be a suitably timbered shed open at one side, into which we groped our way. It was dry and out of the rain, so each of us rolled up in a blanket and although the ground felt a bit bumpy, we were soon off to sleep. During the night I was half conscious of a fair amount of activity. Things ran over me and dreamily I thought it was probably settlement cats, but with the coming of dawn I looked around and discovered we were sleeping on a covered rubbish dump. The place was alive with rats!

Early in the morning we heard the slow, laboured puffing of a goods train approaching and soon it came bustling into the siding. With a lot of snorting, whistling and screeching of brakes, it came to a halt. It was now broad daylight — no time to fiddle with a tarpaulin. It might move straight off again. We ran to the back of the train, well clear of the driver and station master, and clambered into a low sided wagon, then lay on our backs against the platform side to escape detection. The train started to move off in jerks and I was just starting to thank St. Christopher for his timely benediction upon the waifs and strays of this world, when it stopped again with our wagon just outside the station master's office. This was, to say the least, an uncomfortable situation to be in. I watched events apprehensively through a chink in the side of the wagon. The station master came out, casually looked into our truck, not batting an eyelid when he saw Joe and me, then stood with his back to us while he waited for the driver and the guard. They stood chatting for a while, then the driver and guard started to move off to their respective ends of the train.

'Better clear the trucks before you move off!' the station master called, then sat on the side of our wagon, while we could hear the others being turfed out. 'Check under any loose tarpaulins,' he called again.

Eventually we heard the guard call back that his end was clear. The station master shouted to the driver, 'Clear at your end?'

'Yes, all clear.'

'Right,' and with a wave of his hand, we moved off again. As it cleared the siding and moved into bush country, we sat up.

Joe shouted to me above the roar of the wheels and the rattling of the bogie, 'Did you say you believed in St. Christopher?'

'Yes,' I shouted back. 'Well, a gold braided hat suits him.'

During another hold up in a wheat growing area, we strolled around while waiting for another goods train. As far as the eye could see was a vast expanse of ripening wheat and never had I seen such a beautiful sight. As the soft breezes drifted over, they laid the ripening heads sideways to the sun and the effect was like clouds of brilliant gold drifting across the crop. I could have stood looking forever, it was so spellbinding.

There must have been sheep stations in the area too, for when we returned to the siding a farmer came up to us.

'You chaps like some work?' This seemed like a gift from the blue.

'Sure!'

'Right, I'll pay you if you'll load forty bales of wool onto the trucks.'

We jumped to it. The bales had been dumped at the sides of the empty rail wagons. They weighed four hundredweight each and had to be crowbarred up the ramps, then stacked two deep in the trucks. At midday the farmer sauntered over from the saloon and handed over a couple of shillings. 'Have some dinner, chaps,' he said in a big way, 'and I'll pay you when the job's done.' We went into a tumbledown café next to the saloon and had a two course meal for ninepence each, then got on with the job. By about six in the evening we had finished; two wagons loaded up. We sat by the wagons waiting for the return of our employer. At seven o'clock we made a fruitless search for him around the parked lorries and sulkies, then went into the saloon. There was no signs of him there either.

'Anyone seen the owner of wool bales, B stroke N 24?' shouted Joe to the crowd milling around the bar.

'Ay,' someone answered, 'that's Bob Newman's parcel.'

'Any chance of making contact with him. Know where he is?'

'Not a chance, cobbers, passed him going out in his station- waggon about four o'clock and he lives sixty odd miles away. He won't be back!'

If it hadn't been such hard work loading up the bales, we would have tipped them all out again, but such is the fortune of the road.

Eventually, we arrived in Perth and were welcomed by the 'Army' staff like returning heroes. For a shilling a night, we were given bed and breakfast, a room with two beds and all amenities, use of bathroom, lounge, dining room and our room cleaned and beds made daily. In fact the whole place was extremely well run and the 'Army' in every way proved to be friendly, practical and truly Christian.

It is not widely known, but the founder of the Salvation Army, General Booth, was a vegetarian. Many say this was because of stomach trouble, but this is not borne out in his treatise which he sent out to his leaders, *Orders and Regulations of the Officers of the Salvation Army*, in which he has this to say about food. 'It is a great delusion to suppose that flesh meat of any kind is essential to health. Considerably more than three parts of the work of the world is done by men who never taste anything but vegetables, farinaceous food and that of the simplest kind. There are far more strength-producing properties in wholemeal flour, peas, beans, lentils, oatmeal, roots and other vegetables of the same class, than there are in beef, mutton, poultry or fish, or animal food of any description whatever.'

I always feel sorry for great leaders and visionaries like William Booth, for although they see all the evils involved in flesh-eating, they must tread warily on this touchy subject. For although people will die for their faith and sing with gusto their praises to the Lord, yet dare to touch the food on their plates and they will vanish like the dew on the mountain.

Mrs Booth, his no less brilliant partner, worked tirelessly for the down and out women and was also opposed to people living like predators, for in her book *The Treatment of Inebriates* she writes, 'A very significant fact is that when the craving for stimulants is upon a woman, she also longs for animal food. When once the truth has dawned upon her; when once she has seen that by eating meat she strengthens the desire to drink alcohol, if she be sincere, her co-operation is secured... Cases are often received in so bad a state that, under the old regime, we should have expected them to need bed and medicine for weeks before they could be pulled together, but now, with the aid of diet, they are up and about in less than a fortnight... It is a painful glimpse into the selfishness of human nature to find so many friends and relatives who cannot, even for the sake of their loved ones, become abstainers from alcohol and the mere suggestion that their diet should be changed is often greeted with derision... It seems that people who take infinite trouble about their clothing, their reading and many other matters of less importance, are content to consume any food provided it suits their palates, without giving a thought to its properties or purity. If parents can be induced to bring up their children on a pure and simple fruit and vegetable diet, and for their sakes to abolish all that is harmful from the home, I think the need for inebriate homes and all other apparatus for rescuing human wrecks will disappear.'

Humans are only part of the universe, not separate from it. I have seen dogs in Australia chase rabbits, kangaroos and emus. As they go in for the kill, the dogs build up a terrific fury and are the embodiment of hate, for in order to kill, it is essential to possess hate. I do believe that the same emotion is generated in flesh-eating humans. As long as people are predacious, so they will have the killer instinct in them. We have murder, brutality, mugging, baby-battering, wars, religious intolerance, the vast build up of armaments for destruction. All this is now part of our nature because we kill and abuse other forms of life and neither Church nor State will ever reform this degrading trait in humanity — only the reform of our diet.

'Call anytime at the Citadel in Hay Street,' we were told by the elderly couple in charge of the hostel, 'and ask for Ensign Golding, she'll fix you up.' We had of course asked about the chance of a job on our arrival. Next morning we went as directed to the Citadel and made ourselves known to 'Ensign' as we soon found she was known. She welcomed us like long lost relatives. 'I've nothing in at the moment for two, brothers,' she told us, 'but call every day and something suitable is sure to turn up.' In less than a week she had good news for us. A clearing contract at a place called Gutha, about four hundred miles north of Perth. Although we didn't know much about the country around that area, the price offered sounded good. Ensign asked how we were for money and blankets. We had hardly any money left and our blankets had been pawned. 'Well, brothers,' she said, 'the Army in a case like this pays your fare on the train in the form of vouchers and after a meal in the dining room you will each be given two blankets and two pounds for food and incidentals.' With the immediate prospect of comparative wealth, we were on our feet once more, but I felt a bit guilty. Joe, as I well knew, had come out to Australia on their scheme. Perhaps she was under the impression that I had too. I spoke up.

'Mind, Ensign, I think in fairness I should let you know that I'm not a Salvationist.'

'That makes no difference,' she promptly replied, 'You are a child of God!'

I was pleased with her reply. For two pounds and a couple of blankets, I was pleased to be anyone's child — even Frankenstein's.

In the Wheatlands

We rode in style up to Gotha. A few got into the carriage with provisions for a long journey: sandwiches, pies, cakes and bottles of beer, for trains just amble on, stopping at sidings to load or unload, also stopping at desolate farms to either take on or deposit a passenger. One man staggered in, followed by a young woman who was seeing him off.

'Don't forget what I told you, Dad,' she whispered, 'Behave yourself and don't buy any more beer at the sidings.'

He looked sozzled already and vacantly gazed around with bleary eyes. As soon as she left, he was drinking again. Soon after the train moved off and the beer had started flowing, the carriage was resounding to boisterous singing. It always interested me to note how our mood can change. Sometimes I have preferred to be quiet on a train — English style, I suppose — and then someone would start to sing a popular song, another would join in, then another. I would groan inwardly then reluctantly join in 'just to please', then warm to it and suddenly get in the mood and sing with abandon as lustily as the rest. There's something infectious about singing and it suits the free and easy temperament of the Australians. They are good bosses too. I'll give you an instance.

Later, when a contract had finished, I had word that a 'cocky' (wheat) farmer wanted another hand for harvesting. We were playing pontoon in the siding when we heard about it. Those card schools, by the way, lasted from about three o'clock Saturday afternoon to the early hours of Monday morning — non stop. Anyway, I was to be introduced to Alan Butler at the next bush dance. Wally Wright was the 'banker' and while shuffling the cards remarked, 'By the way, Wilf, if he asks if you are experienced in harvesting, just say 'Yes' because all the equipment simply takes a bit of common sense to get the hang of and the others will soon put you wise, but don't accept less then two pounds ten a week (keep was always included), because that is what the others are getting.'

At the dance on the following Saturday night I was introduced to the farmer, a bulky, friendly Australian.

'I believe you're looking for a job?' he asked.

'That's right. Any chance of helping with the harvest?'

'Yes, I do want another hand. Experienced with a header?'

'Oh, yes,' I answered casually.

'What height do you cut?'

While I didn't even know what the thing looked like, this question was, to say the least, baffling. 'Well,' I answered trying to look knowledgeable but thinking hard, 'I vary the height.' This answer, I found out later, wasn't too bad because the operator alters the height to suit the crop. The 'header' is like a long horizontal corkscrew revolving in a curved base serrated on the lower edge. As the teeth go through the crop, the huge revolving corkscrew snaps off the wheat heads and feeds them into the thresher.

'What time in the morning do you start?'

'About eight usually.' This answer was hopeless. It's impossible to start work before nine o'clock or even later. You have to wait until the sun has dried the dew off the crop. Before this, the straw is as tough as string, but once it is dry it is quite brittle and snaps off under the rollers.

Alan, being a typical Aussie, didn't bat an eyelid. He would have done the same in my position. 'How about two pounds a week and you'll be taught how to work a header and drive a tractor?' Now to undercut other workers is the most unforgivable sin in Australia and I had been told what the others were getting, so there was no excuse.

'No, the deal's off, two pounds ten or nothing doing.' Probably he guessed I'd been primed. 'Right. How about two pounds a week for the first fortnight while you learn how to use the harvesting machinery and then two ten?' This sounded fair enough to me because after all, I was a greenhorn. It was settled and Alan Butler turned out to be a good boss. In fact we became firm friends and although there were six other men, we always worked together. He drove the tractor while I manipulated the huge header being pulled behind. In the distance, through the shimmering heat, we could see clouds of dust billowing up from where the other teams were working in the scorching sun. What with the noise from the tractor and the banging of the header as the wheat was being threshed, the din was terrific. Speech or even shouting to each other was out of the question, yet in a very short time we could pass simple messages by sign language. The first I learned was when he put his hands on his hips and swayed his backside, meaning a woman was in sight. I soon got the hang of harvesting: when the straw was brittle enough to work, how to manipulate the header according to the varying height of the crop and also how to dodge the seed pod of the mustard plants without missing too much of the grain.

We were a happy bunch and our appetites were enormous. I often wondered if there was any profit left for the boss after we had satisfied our constant hunger. His wife had no help, yet meal after meal was always abundant and smack on time. She was a terrific worker and loved the extra company at harvest time. We had our own outhouse for sleeping, but we went into the house for meals.

One thing always grieved me and that was the pastime of some of the men catching budgerigars. They used to smear a strong glue on the branches of trees and when a bird got stuck, they would climb and pick it off. Although at that time I was unaware of the unity of all life, I still thought it was cruel, for these birds spent the rest of their days in tiny cages in our dark outhouse sitting motionless on the bottom with their beaks open, panting for air in the heat, whereas in their freedom they had chattered while they flew among the foliage, quite happy and colourful.

One morning, after I had been working there for a week, Alan and I were making our way across the wheatfield to the tractor, when he told me I was on two pound ten from the day I started. I suppose there are exceptions, and the average Aussie boss will barter, but he is fair.

Tom Dully

Let me return to the work we were originally bound for in Gutha. We arrived at Tom Dully's place late at night, footsore and weary after walking five or six miles along bush tracks from leaving the siding. From a long way off we had been guided by the flickering light from a solitary log fire in a distant valley. We were quite close to a man reading a book by the firelight before he became aware of our presence. 'Tom Dully?' we enquired.

'That's right, come to do some clearing for me?'

'Yes, sent up from the Salvation Army in Perth.' He was obviously pleased to see us. Probably was glad to have company and someone to talk to.

'You must be tired, chaps,' he said jumping up. 'Dump your swags and I'll knock up a meal for you.' We sat by the fire on a log that Tom had vacated and in next to no time were sipping a mug of tea, while Tom set to preparing a meal of bacon and eggs with fried bread. His welcome really gladdened us and nothing would induce him to sleep in his shack. Both of us must accept the shelter of his home and he would sleep by the fire, rolled in a blanket. He was, as I said, delighted with the prospect of company and gave us a real colonial welcome.

At daybreak he came back into the shack with more tea — Aussies are great tea drinkers — then he busied himself making breakfast and intermittently asked questions as he came in and out. Were we short of tobacco or papers? No, we were all right for smokes. Had we been to any political meetings in Perth? No, but we had seen one or two good variety shows. Had we seen any of the labour ministers? No, only Salvation Army lassies. Had we any idea who would get in at the next election? Did we not have time to go to a meeting? No, not really, but we had been to one of the Army's open air meetings and every time a Salvationist shouted 'Hallelujah,' a youth in the crowd had shouted back, 'I'm a bum!' Our interests seemed to be at variance. After breakfast, we borrowed an axe, felled a few saplings and with some old corrugated iron sheets and hessian bags from Tom, built ourselves a shack.

The money that Tom offered for the clearing and which we accepted was quite fair, for the thickest trunks of the jarrahs and strip-barks were no more than a foot in diameter with a few 'blackboys' and not much under-growth. Blackboys are a tough, thick black trunked 'grass tree' about six feet high with a tuft of fronds at the top. They yield the fragrant resin known as Botany Bay gum. If you wrote home to England and said you had spent the morning 'chopping off the heads of blackboys', it was prudent to add an explanation.

We didn't need a crosscut saw as all the felling could be done by axe and each worked in half chain widths the length of the area to be cleared.

One week, Joe would stay behind at the shack after breakfast to clear up and to prepare the dinner, and the next week it would be my turn. It was early one morning, when Joe was left at the camp, that I had an insight into the quick reflexes of the human body when confronted with sudden danger. With the axe over my shoulder and swishing a spray of leaves about my head to keep the swarm of flies away, I stepped over the felled timber, making for the standing trees where we had finished felling the previous evening, when I nearly stepped on a deadly brown-spotted snake. Obviously, it had been sunning itself and heard me coming. I had stepped over a fallen trunk and my foot was descending right onto the snake before I realised the danger. It was coiled with its head raised in the centre of the coil, ready to strike. The next thing I knew was that I had taken a jump of four or five feet right over it — and from a standing position, on one leg! I looked around and watched it glide into a hole under the trunk. Later on I was busy felling before Joe arrived, when I had a feeling of sickness. I got a bit worried, because sickness is the first reaction to a snake bite. Had it been quicker than me? But there was no sign of a bite on my legs. Probably, as I jumped, I had swallowed a few flies and this has the same effect, but it was the speed of the body's reaction to danger that amazed me when I thought about it.

After a few days, Tom, for some obscure reason, took a dislike to Joe. Nothing offensive, for Tom was always polite, but the aversion soon became obvious. He came over to our shack two or three times a week in the evening and we soon noticed that his conversation was directed at me in particular. If Joe had anything to say, Tom waited patiently until he had finished, then continued to talk to me. Later on, after a masculine display of superiority over a difference of opinion, Tom became Joe's best friend. I'll tell you about it later.

Tom, though, I'm sorry to say it, was turning a bit odd in his ways. He had been a colonel or major in the first world war and as well as having an air of authority about him, he possessed a brilliant brain. Every time he came to visit us he talked politics, a subject he never seemed to tire of, and always before he left asked if we had any reading matter. We received a batch of papers sent out from home now and again and at times gave him two or three newspapers and a book. A couple of nights later he would return them and asked if we had any more. Once or twice we quizzed him, thinking he couldn't possibly have read them; but he had. Not only had he read them, but names, facts, and the smallest details had sunk in too. We've seen him after midnight and a hard day's work, still avidly reading by the flickering firelight from his log fire.

But the lonely life in the bush was having an adverse effect on our employer. A quiet, friendly man used to work for him at times, but neither of us could fathom out where he lived. His wife used to come at midday with a meal for him and a more friendly, inoffensive couple it would be hard to meet. Yet sometimes, when Tom spoke to Joe and me, he would suddenly walk away and look behind a tree to make sure this man, Jim, wasn't eavesdropping! Why he thought anyone would hide behind a tree, listening to a political monologue, puzzled me. It was a pity that such a cultured and intelligent man should have this twist. We guessed that this had something to do with his attitude to Joe.

An episode that happened at the end of the contract had its humour although, at the time, tempers ran high. Joe was over six feet tall and like many big men, had a soft heart. During the felling we came to a small tree in which a bird sat on eggs. If we went near, it crouched low on the eggs with beak open, as much as to say, 'You dare!' Neither of us had the heart to betray such maternal courage, so left the tree standing.

Now the terms of a contract, although only a 'gentleman's agreement', stipulate that all the timber must be layed. When we had finished, Tom came with us one morning to measure up the acreage. The unfelled tree in the centre of the clearing stuck out like a sore thumb.

'You've still got a tree to fell,' said Tom.

I told him we had left it because a bird was sitting on eggs. Tom didn't see it our way. 'The tree must be felled before I measure up.'

'You heard what Wilf said,' cut in Joe and turned red. 'There's eggs being hatched in that tree and no one is felling it. Neither we — you — nor anyone else!'

'All right,' said Tom, 'No money — the contract's not finished.'

Joe was in battle mood now. 'Not only has that tree not to be felled, but no burning off has to be done either, until those eggs are hatched.' The difference in opinion gained in anger and momentum until the two men were standing face to face and on the point of coming to blows. Tom eventually backed down. If it had come to a fight, he would have fared worst for, although he was big and tough, Joe was much younger and fighting fit. 'Right,' agreed Tom, 'I'll pay, but under duress.' He evidently realised that discretion was the better part of valour in this case, but what amused me during the altercation was the fact that the bird causing the upheaval was only the size of a sparrow!

It is little episodes like this that prove to me our inherent unity with all life, but a scar over our finer feelings has hardened into a near impenetrable crust because of flesh-eating and a callous disregard for other forms of life. It's the same as sinking a piece of clear crystal into the ocean for a time. On being retrieved it would be unrecognisable, because of the encrustations of marine life, yet the pure crystal would still be there. The only way we can regain our lost clarity is by returning to a non-harming, non-killing Edenic diet.

However, there was no lasting malice. In fact, the very opposite, for Tom came over to our shack in the evening and after paying for the work, offered us another contract. We agreed to go with him the next day and fix a price after seeing the area to be cleared. 'By the way, Joe,' said Tom, 'I had a safety razor sent as a present. Would it be any use to you? I always use an open razor,' and he produced from his pocket a new razor in a case. It had an adjustable cutting edge and a strap for sharpening. From then on, all his coolness to Joe was forgotten.

Next day we went to see the area to be cleared. It was just short of ten acres, with some half dozen redgums to the acre but little undergrowth. The redgums were big, at least four feet in diameter, and would need to be 'scarved' and crosscut. Tom offered four pounds an acre which sounded fair enough, so we accepted.

Joe left early the next morning with the axe to start scarving. To use the crosscut saw that Tom had loaned us would need both of us on the job, but meanwhile it was my turn to clean up after breakfast and peel the potatoes ready for dinner. An hour or so later I was busy sharpening my axe on the carborundum, when Joe emerged from the surrounding bush. By the broad smile on his face, I could see he was the bearer of good news. Alluvial gold has been found at times in unlikely places in Australia. Had he tripped over a lump of gold? 'Wilf,' he called as soon as he got within earshot, 'we're in the money!'

'How come, Joe?' I asked, getting excited at the prospect of wealth.

'Those redgums are hollow. I took a swipe at the first and the axe shot out of my hands, straight through the hollow centre. There's only the bark and four or five inches of soft sap wood. The rest is hollow. I've cleared an acre already!' A laughing jackass in a neighbouring tree suddenly shattered the silence. Those birds always remind me of the witch in a pantomime when she has just carried out some dastardly act. Its raucous cackle filled the air and echoed through the forest. Was this one laughing at us, or was it laughing at Tom?

'Joe,' I said, when the din had died down, 'We must be crafty here or Tom might cancel the contract if he finds out.'

'Yes,' he agreed, 'but if we do an acre a day, we'll pick up forty pounds in a couple of weeks, then have another spell in Perth.'

We went back to the clearing and I stood spellbound for a while. Sure enough, Joe had felled half a dozen huge trees in an hour. Giant redgums were lying all over the place. It must have been a poor subsoil for although the trees looked solid enough as they stood, their trunks were just shells. We cleared some brushwood, then went back to the camp and got changed and went to the siding where there was always the chance of joining a card school or some other diversion. It was a long walk but it filled in the day and we had already earned four pounds which, in those days, was good money for a day's work. With our present luck we could earn twenty pounds a week, even spreading the work out.

It was late in the evening when we got back and after kindling the fire, we made a stew from salt pork, beans, and potatoes, then after the usual mug of tea, rolled ourselves cigarettes and sat by the fire in the bright moonlight, at peace with the world. It was very late when Tom came over to join us, but as he was busy harvesting with a five horse team at the time, he never turned in before the early hours anyway, so we weren't particularly surprised. He was always polite and formal.

'Mind if I join you?'

'Not at all, Tom. Take a seat.'

He sat on a log, took a solid chunk of tobacco from a tin, laid it on the hot embers for a few seconds to soften it, then studiously cut shavers off and, after filling and lighting his pipe, sat thoughtfully smoking.

'Jim been over today?' Joe asked, but Tom remained silent, lost in thought. After a while he took his pipe and carefully tapped out the hot ashes on a stone. Suddenly he broke the silence. 'Sorry, chaps, the contract's finished. I've been over to the clearing. The trees are hollow. I'll give you a pound an acre if you want to carry on but no more.'

'But Tom,' I remonstrated, 'an agreement cannot be broken like that. We admit it's money for old rope, but we didn't know that when the price was fixed.' But Tom wouldn't give in and we wouldn't accept a lower price, so after being paid for the acre next day, we packed our kit and were off.

We were surprised that Tom, being an Australian, took the attitude he did, for they are usually good gamblers and accept their losses with the same 'sang-froid' as their wins. Tom had lost on the deal and reneged. So now we knew who the jackass had been laughing at!

Bag sewing

Back at the siding that evening we called in at the bar looking for work. We both struck lucky. The harvest had just been gathered and a couple of cockies wanted bag sewers. We would have to part though, because the quantities were small, both were parcels of between two and three thousand at ten shillings (50p) a hundred.

Usually, the farms are near the railway for convenience of transport and my employer lived just a couple of miles away. He certainly wasn't a prosperous farmer, for when I went out next day, I found him living in a most gloomy shack. It had a roof of rusty corrugated iron sheets, with old wheat bags sewn together for both inner and outer walls. He and his wife were certainly more productive than the surrounding land, for the place was swarming with shy children peeping around from behind the sacking, for they seldom saw strangers. But the heat! What with the pitiless sun shining on the iron roof and the sacking preventing any flow of air, it was stifling. I was glad to get outside.

He took me about half a mile along a dense bush track, then as it veered left between an outcrop of high boulders, the huge wheatfield came into view. Afar off, emus and kangaroos stood motionless in the stubble, looking our way, for they have marvellous sight and hearing. As we stood surveying the field, one kangaroo slowly loped away in the shimmering heat, then an emu moved towards the safety of the bush and soon it turned into a general stampede. Emus are funny birds. Often, near a fence, one will start to walk along it, another will join it, then another and for no apparent reason the rest seem to take a sudden fright and in a matter of seconds the whole flock is racing along in senseless terror. If the fence turns inwards, their speed is so fast that they cannot take the bend and pile on top of one another. Hundreds used to die in this way.

The wheat bags to be sewn were stacked ready filled around the field, but as it was by now near sunset I looked for somewhere to camp down for the night after the farmer had left. In the surrounding bush I came upon the remains of an old mud shack. There was no roof, just the crumbling walls three or four feet high with one or two doors still hanging on rusty hinges. I decided to use it and rigged up a tripod bed of saplings and wheat bags in what had been a room. I lit a fire outside and, after a meal of flapjacks with beans, decided to turn in.

The moonlight was bright enough to read by, so I rummaged around some rubbish by an old stove and found a faded red backed book with the intriguing title *When the Time Comes*. It turned out to be a book on childbirth and scared the wits out of me. Whoever wrote that book should have taken a course in psychology first, for it gave, in dragged out detail, all the preparation and pain to expect. After a while, as I wasn't likely to become an expectant mother, I threw it back towards the stove, pulled the blanket over my head to keep out the bright moonlight and lay listening to night sounds of the bush, which seemed to accentuate the stillness and desolation. Now and then a distant dingo howled plaintively and the occasional twig snapping and thumping caused by roaming kangaroos but, lulled by the croaking of countless frogs, I was soon asleep.

Suddenly, I wakened again with a start. Someone was standing by the side of the bed! My muscles tightened, but I kept up a rhythmic breathing, feigning sleep, as various possibilities raced through my mind. Had a swaggie seen the glow from my fire and come over to investigate? There were thirty pounds in my hip pocket. After all, I didn't know the farmer. Was he to be trusted? Although my head was still covered by the blanket, I knew where the watcher stood. Quick action was my only chance of self defence. In one lightning move I whipped the blanket away, swung my legs onto the ground and sat looking into the eyes of — a kangaroo! For a few seconds we sat like a motionless tableau in the moonlight, then it slowly shuffled round, jumped over the wall and disappeared into the bush.

These animals are very inquisitive and this one, seeing the queer contraption that happened to be my bed, had paused to investigate. What puzzled me, after my heart had stopped racing, was what instinct had not only aroused me from deep sleep, but also let me know the exact position of the intruder. There must be some primordial part of us that never sleeps.

While on the subject, another thing that baffles me is that I have come in dog tired, fallen asleep in an easy chair and immediately been off chasing butterflies over a meadow or some such daft energetic fantasy, without the least feeling of fatigue. Fatigue must only affect the muscles and the part of the brain that motivates them. Another curious point is that you can, in a dream, be in completely strange surroundings and mixing with people you have never met, yet never question how you got there. In the dream, it all seems perfectly normal and real. Recently, in a dream, I was walking with a woman who had her arm linked in mine. We knew each other intimately. As she was speaking, I was studying her face and thinking, 'She still has the residuum left of the beauty she had in her youth.' I knew her better than my own sister. When I wakened, I could still see her face quite plainly, yet I didn't know the woman from Adam, or rather from Eve. I'd certainly never set eyes on her in my life. Some say this is because of reincarnation and you have known people in a previous life. There may be some truth in this explanation because I can still remember, as a tiny baby, looking around and thinking, 'Oh, I'm back in the world again.' The world certainly wasn't new to me.

The Captain's place

Allow me to return to my story. I was duly paid at the end of the bag sewing and any thoughts of the cocky trying to rob me in my sleep were far from just. In fact, he called on me quite a few times during the period I was there to replenish my stores and to refill the kerosene tins with water. He was the usual good Australian employer. After the job and bags had been paid up and sewn up, it was back to the siding to try and contact Joe. When I got there in the late afternoon, there was no sign of Joe hanging around, so I went over to the store and was stocking up for a couple of days' rations when a smart, fresh complexioned man came in. He looked like a sea-faring type and had an air of authority. He was buying pipe twist when I left, but caught me up as I left the veranda steps.

'You and a cobber work for Tom Dully lately?'

'Yes, cleared some land for him.'

'I'm Captain Bullied and know Tom well, we both came out to the wheat belt about the same time, but I had a bit more cash than Tom and bought an established place. Know anything about poultry?'

'Yes, worked on dairy farms in the South-West.'

'Now the harvest's over, I want someone to look after the place while I go on holiday.'

'What's the job?' I enquired.

'Looking after some poultry — a few hens and turkeys and doing some straw burning. I'll be away six weeks. Nothing to it really.'

After the harvest in Australia, the wheat stalks left standing are quite long, for the headers only snap the grains off, leaving the straw to be fire ringed and burnt.

'What's the money?'

'Three pounds a week, with food provided and of course you'll live in the bungalow.'

'Sounds all right to me Captain. When will you want me?'

'Any time you like, the sooner the better.' Evidently Tom Dully had turned up trumps and spoken well of us, because a farmer naturally wants someone he can trust to leave in charge. I told him that I wanted to meet up with my mate, Joe, and it might be a couple of days before he came to the siding.

'I'll be back again at the week end for rations.'

'Right. I'll probably have seen him by then.' The Captain went over to a Nash car where a dog was barking excitedly at his approach and after revving up, he was away in a cloud of dust.

Joe came in early the next morning. He had also got fixed up again with a Cornish immigrant farmer. I met him later, an elderly, thin, tough man, hard as iron but straight as a die. The Captain came in again on the Saturday. I introduced him to Joe and, after a friendly chat, threw my few belongings into the back of the car and we were off.

'What part of the Old Country are you from?' he asked as we headed for a track leading through the bush.

'Newcastle.'

'Oh! a Geordie!'

The dog, a medium sized, short haired, alert animal sat between us looking straight ahead through the windscreen during the journey. I could tell it was very conscious of the presence of a stranger. Later on she and I, for it was a bitch, had some good times together out hunting in the bush.

'Handy having a dog, out in the bush alone, Captain.'

'Geordie,' he replied, taking one hand off the wheel and giving it an affectionate pat, 'I love her like a sister! She's obedient, loyal and a good guard to have around the place. I wouldn't part with her for a fortune. she's a real companion.'

I like cats.

'Got a cat?'

'Yes.' The car weaved and skidded along the sandy track, with the wheels nearly locked in the deep ruts. From the dark tunnel like track, hemmed in by thick scrub and overhead trees, we emerged suddenly into brilliant sunshine as we passed by the side of a wheatfield, then drove into dense bush again, finally emerging into a clearing in which there was a good sized bungalow. Two or three rather dilapidated poultry houses with high wire meshed runs nearby were rather an eyesore, but surrounding the bungalow a garden of roses and tamarisk, interspaced with lemon bushes, greatly relieved the general appearance of the place. Lemon bushes, with their bright yellow fruit set in dark, glossy green leaves always reminded me of lit-up Christmas trees, for in the sunlight the lemons have an iridescent glow that is truly beautiful. Surrounding the clearing was the inevitable bush with its scent of wild blossom mixed with a strange elusive odour of death and decay. For the bush is still primordial forest in which rebirth follows death in an endless cycle and this applies not only to the vegetation but to the birds and animals that inhabit it. Some of the early settlers made the mistake of clearing all the land adjacent to their dwellings in an ever widening circle and eventually had to make wide treks across the outlying paddocks to procure firewood; a waste of both time and labour, for wood is the only heating fuel. The Captain, with a wide belt of bush around his bungalow, was assured of not only of heating, but protection from the occasional gales that spring up in the winter.

The first thing he did on alighting from the car, was to put 'Dog' (as he called the bitch!) on a leash, then attach the leash to a big metal ring on a raised wire stretched between two poles about twenty-five yards apart, so the dog had exercise but not liberty. A garage set at right angles to the far side of the bungalow, housed a new, gleaming Chevrolet truck. The Captain got back in the car and parked it alongside.

'Geordie!' he called as he got out and eyed the truck as if it was some obstacle still to be overcome, 'If you go into the siding while I'm away, use the car, because I've just had the truck sent up from Perth. I haven't even tried it yet.' He came over and led the way up the veranda steps and we went into the bungalow. It was, as I had expected, all clean and shipshape inside. From a hook above the wash basin he took an old oval shaped pilchard fish tin and into it mixed two raw eggs with some bran.

'Now,' he said, 'come outside and see how obedient Dog is.' When he emerged, it was obvious that she was famished, for with strained leash and taut with excitement she waited for the food. Captain put the tin right under her nose. She stood motionless with saliva dripping from her mouth, awaiting permission to eat. 'Right!' said her master, as he gave a nod at the same time. She pounced on the food and in a matter of seconds was licking and licking away, trying to extract the last morsel from an empty tin, as it skidded along the ground. 'How's that for obedience?' he asked, glowing with pride.

Later, we sat down to quite a good meal of cold pork with pickled onions and potatoes, followed by Cape Gooseberry jam on bread. The bread was a bit tough. He had probably made it himself and probably knocked hell out of the dough. After the meal, I was shown two tins, and he explained in most emphatic terms, that one was for beef dripping and the other for lard.

'Whatever you do, Geordie, don't mix the dripping with the lard,' he said with some concern, as if the union would cause some explosion or friction between the ghosts of the dead animals.

'Right, Captain.'

'And when you have a meal, be sure to clear every crumb away off the table and floor, or the place will be swarming with ants in next to no time.'

'Right, Captain.' I was beginning to feel really nautical with all this 'Right, Captain' and 'Yes, Captain.'

'We'll go out and see the poultry now.'

I sprang to attention. 'Yes, Captain.' He had a few brown leghorns and about thirty turkeys and his method of husbandry seemed a bit strange. He tried to feed one turkey with mash mixed with olive oil on a dessert spoon. It was, explained the Captain, suffering from the heat and olive oil was the only cure, but the bird was reluctant to accept the proferred food and the Captain, on his hands and knees, with the spoon held out at arm's length was trying to gain the confidence of the patient by uttering the most unusual coo-ing sounds. As he crawled forward, the bird moved back and seemed more interested in the antics of the man than the elixir on the spoon. The final act had the Captain flat on his stomach still intent upon conquest.

Captain Bullied turned out to be an odd sort of farmer in more ways than one. He had been a Captain on the Steam Packet Line and like the majority of seafaring men, his monotonous pacing of the bridge had been illuminated with visions of becoming a super farmer when he had saved enough money. He had worked out schemes that would enhance the whole agricultural process and, the more he day-dreamed, the more erratic became his ideas. Farming and stock books had been avidly read and in his mental excursions into fantasy, backed up by technical knowledge, he saw rippling acres of super grain and lush meadows with fat cattle, all enhanced by his master touch.

I know this was true, not only from what he told me, but I had a sea captain brother smitten with the same bug. They all had the daft idea that they would make, not only first class farmers, but grow crops the like no one had seen before. This captain proved to be no exception, but theories seldom work out in practice and this applies especially to farming, where trial and error with local soil and weather conditions is the only criterion. I heard later that the first year he took over the farm the seed was planted far too deep and the shoots roamed around the bowels of the earth looking for the light — and only half of them found it. The next year, realising his mistake, he went to the other extreme and barely covered them, so what the birds and mice didn't eat came up. However, I should imagine that he was a good sea captain, for in the evening after the poultry had been fed and locked in their enclosures and the warm glow from the oil lamp lit up the room, he showed me photos of him taken on board ship and a smart man he looked in his uniform with its display of gold braid and surrounded by officers from the upper deck. He had, as I mentioned, been on the Steam Packet Line but had left to put his pipe dreams into practice and become a farmer. I asked him if he had been a strict disciplinarian. 'Well,' he answered, 'I was strict, but fair. I always liked to think of my ship as a happy ship.' Funny, when I'd asked my brother the same question once, I got the same reply. Probably they were both right, for usually men don't mind strict discipline, providing it's impartial.

A few days later, I drove the Captain into the siding to catch the train for Perth and the first thing I did on my return was to let the dog have her freedom, for to deprive any living creature of its freedom is both cruel and thoughtless. She loved being released and although it was hot in the afternoon sun, for the Captain had taken me around in the morning to show me the paddocks to be burned, she raced around for a full half hour in sheer ecstasy.

Strange events

For the next couple of weeks, events followed one another in rapid succession. The very next day, I was sitting on the veranda after dinner when I heard the dog barking furiously in the direction of the enclosures, but as she was such a lively dog, I took little notice. Once or twice she came to the veranda steps barking urgently and was off again. The third time she came, I knew something must be wrong, so I followed. Dog ran to one of the enclosures, then back to me, as much as to say, 'This way! This way!' As I got near, I could see the turkeys flying around in wild terror — and no wonder, for inside was a huge eagle hawk with a turkey in its talons. It had obviously flown into the enclosure, seized a turkey, but with the weight of its victim, it couldn't gain height to clear the ten foot wire meshing. Bird and turkey were locked together and covered in dust.

Each time the eagle hawk made a strenuous effort to clear the wire surround, it was just short of height and fell back to earth. Eagle hawks, by the way, cannot release a victim from their talons, unless in free flight. I opened the wire gate to let Dog in. She ran in, then changed her mind and ran out again, bewildered by all the commotion. All the other turkeys were flying around in panic. Dog was obviously scared and looked at me as much as to say, 'You try!' I grasped a long axe handle and ventured in, feeling a slight pang of pity as I approached the huge bird. Because of its burden, the wild, beautiful, majestic bird was completely at my mercy. As it lay helpless against the wire with its curved and evil-looking beak open, I noticed that its eyes turned completely around with fear. The iris disappeared and the eye turned white as if it was trying to shut out the sight of its predicament. It had to be killed and with one well aimed blow, I did the trick.

The turkey, when released from the talons, was breathing its last and died within minutes. I measured the eagle and it was over six feet from wing tip to wing tip. The talons and legs were cruel looking too. Fur, not feathers, came down from the shank right to the claws, which were three inches long and curved inwards. It has to pull these talons apart to release its prey and that is why it can only be done in flight.

Turkeys are beautiful birds and very gentle. They always remind me of well bred ladies. The Captain had told me that if any became affected by the heat, to administer olive oil from a spoon and, sure enough, one or two were overcome nearly every day. I would find them lying on the ground with beaks open and long necks laid out in a posture of extreme lassitude. Sitting on a log, I took them in turn between my knees, gently opened their beaks and administered small drops of olive oil from a spoon, then in a shady place, made a depression in the ground, damped it with water, then sat a turkey in it to recover. After a couple of days' treatment they usually started to take an interest in life.

Once, while I was intent on this job, Dog came dashing up in her usual boisterous manner, barked like mad, then was off again. I was intent on gently pouring oil into the open beak of a turkey when I heard a man's voice calling, 'Will you take this dog away?' Looking up from my task of healing, I saw a swaggie about a hundred yards off and partly concealed by the bright dappling sunlight as it shone through the leaves of the paperbarks, held at bay by the dog. Usually she was very obedient, but when I called her back the only concession she made to my command, was to let the man progress slowly towards me while she backed slowly with hackles raised and barking like mad. Obviously he was nervous of the dog and asked for his water bag to be filled.

I took the bag and as the swaggie followed me to the water tank at the back of the bungalow, Dog walked backwards behind me, facing the stranger, still barking vociferously. I filled the water bag, then put Dog on her run-wire, not only to relieve the man's trepidation but to get some peace myself. As it had now turned midday, I asked him if he would like to stay for dinner. He was pleased to accept and proved to be very well educated and entertaining company. History seemed to be his pet subject and what he didn't know about royalty and the intrigues of Kings and Queens wasn't worth knowing. I liked the man. He struck me as a public school don who had gone to seed. We enjoyed the meal, then before he left to continue on his way, I gave him a supply a meat, bread, butter, tea, sugar and tobacco, enough to last for a couple of days. Just as he was leaving, he asked if the dog was chained up all night. It was, but I thought a 'white lie' might come in handy. 'No,' I answered casually, 'she's got free run all the time.' If he thought the dog was free, he'd never dare return under the cover of darkness if he had any sinister notion in mind — and one never knows!

It was a few days or rather nights after this, that I learnt the peculiarities of poison. There were a few foxes around, for once or twice I heard the screech of bitches during the night and I was afraid that they might attack the poultry, so I went into the siding one evening and purchased some strychnine from the store. The storekeeper gave me instructions on how to use it. It had to be enough, I was told, to cover a threepenny piece — no more, no less — for evidently the amount had to be exact, and a final caution: to be sure to bury any surplus deeply.

Late that same night, after chaining up the dog and making sure the cat was in, I started laying the baits as per instructions. The plan was to have two pieces of meat for each bait. The one with the poison was to lay on top of the ground and the other, without poison, was to be buried six inches below. This ensures, in theory anyway, that the fox dies on the spot; for after eating the surface bait, it smells the buried meat and starts scratching up the earth to get at it. While engaged in this task, the poison is doing its deadly work and the animal collapses and dies on the spot. After supper, I slit open each piece of meat to be poisoned with great care, holding it with a fork, for there must be no smell of human contact, otherwise the fox would get suspicious and move on. I made ten poisoned baits, put Dog on her running lead, looked in the bedroom and saw the cat sound asleep on my bed, then after shutting doors and windows, I set off with spade and baits to lay them at intervals around the poultry houses. It was a beautiful, clear, moonlight night as I busied myself with the distasteful job of spreading death, with only the incessant night chorus of croaking frogs and the occasional hoot of a hunting owl to disturb the peace. However, I eased my conscience with the thought that the job was essential: turkeys and hens being of more use to mankind than foxes. Anyway, it was a case of Hobson's choice.

I had been out for more than an hour and laid eight baits, when something rubbed against my leg — it was the cat! To say I was filled with dismay would be the understatement of the year, for I am particularly fond of cats. It must have had a secret exit from the house, unknown to me. With a heavy heart I retraced my steps over the laid baits to find my worst fears confirmed. He had eaten the lot! Eight lethal doses of strychnine had been consumed. I carried him back to the house full of remorse in the knowledge that I had been very careless. Once inside the house, I gave him some warm diluted condensed milk, which he readily lapped up, then turned in. I left the hurricane lamp burning on the bedside table so that I could render any assistance when the final hour came. The cat jumped onto his usual place at the foot of the bed without any apparent wobble or discomfort. In fact, he revelled in my extra attentions, purring like a dynamo while I kept stroking and rubbing him under the chin before I lay down. Sleep however stayed far from me. I was far too concerned about the cat's welfare. Frequently, I would sit up in bed and look at the cat. In the end the cat thought there must be something wrong with me! Every time I sat up, he opened his eyes and looked back at me with compassion. I stroked him again. He purred again. Then I would lie for about ten minutes, sit up again and have another look. He sat up too and looked at me with soft, silent eyes full of concern. Obviously he thought I was either ill or had gone potty; and so we spent the night, like a couple of yo-yos. Anyway much to my relief, the strychnine had not the slightest effect on the cat.

In the siding lived a schoolmaster who taught in the bush school. He was as thin as a lath, but what he lacked in brawn was certainly made up for in brains, for he was the most intellectual and knowledgeable person I have ever come across. He used to join the card school at the week ends and got plenty of ribbing for his lack of muscle, but for all that he was well liked and a great favourite with the men, as he took the chaffing in good part and was an excellent conversationalist with a vast store of knowledge. I've heard him in conversation about the sailing ships which raced from Australia to England with their holds filled with grain or wool. Tonnage of ship and cargo would be mentioned, type and spread of sail, storms met on the journey, date of arrival after number of days at sea — all would be recounted in detail, and he wasn't speaking to a dumb audience either, for quite a few of us were well versed in these matters. Yet, a little later, he might expound on the chemical action that causes rust, or the lineage of the Tsars of Russia!

Counting on his versatile knowledge, I told him about the cat, for if anyone could answer the riddle, he could. 'Well,' he replied to my question, 'strychnine is obtained from the seeds of the nightshade plant and is put, in very small amounts, into some medicines for muscular and nerve troubles. It is likely your cat had so much that the poison annulled itself. I think this does apply to strychnine.' Whether his answer was correct I cannot say, but the cat never even blinked an eyelid over the experience. The only other solution of which I could think was that some other night prowler, perhaps an owl and not the cat, had eaten the bait, or the cat, having nine lives and only eating eight lethal doses, still had one to go!

I set no more poison baits. To be quite honest, subconsciously, I had a feeling of guilt in doing it. So in the end, as far as I know, no animal suffered from my nefarious midnight work and, further, none of the poultry were killed.

Ants in Australia are a real pest. There are many kinds and the only thing one can say about them is that they are industrious. I wouldn't say that the individual ant is particularly brainy, for I have seen one come to the obstacle of a blade of grass, climb up to the top, down the other side, then carry on again, but as a colony they certainly have a communal sense. Termites, the white ants, build an ant hill up to six, seven, or even more feet in height with the thickest part in line with the circuit of the sun for, being riddled with tunnels, it provides insulation against the heat. The shorter, thin sides face roughly north and south, presumably to catch the draughts of cooler air and this alignment of the ant hill is invariably seen. Before sitting down in the open, it is always a good precaution to cover the ground or to make sure that the area is clear, for if ants get into your clothing, they send you berserk and some, particularly the red and black bull ants, can really bite.

At Mr Peale's place in the south, on one occasion, I was working a mile or so from the homestead, clearing some rough undergrowth, when a bull ant bit my foot. I leapt a yard into the air with the sudden pain, then in feverish haste, I took my boot off in case he took another bite. Shaking out the industrious biter (I hadn't any socks on), I rubbed the bite with saliva, yet even as I rubbed the foot, it swelled up. Tom was hobbled in a clover field near by, so I limped over with one foot bare, for it had swollen so much that it was impossible to get the boot on again, and rode back. Three or four hours elapsed before my foot returned to normal. The Aborigines, as I mentioned before, have the answer to the ant problem, for by rubbing themselves over with iguana fat, the ants avoid them like the plague. It was not only the ants that avoided them — we did too, for the smell of stale grease radiating from the bush natives was enough to knock you over.

While Joe and I worked for Tom Dully, we thought we had the ant menace solved for we put the legs of the beds, tables and chairs in old tobacco tins filled with oil. Yet once, while having a meal, I suddenly noticed an ant on my food. Spooning it up, I flicked it into the open, but when I looked again at the food, two more ants were crawling over it. It was puzzling where they had come from. Then from above, two more ants fell onto the plate. Looking up, I saw a stream of invaders crawling along one of the timber roof supports and when they got directly over the food, they dropped onto it — some three or four feet. Whether they went by smell or saw it, one cannot say, but they certainly had some means of communicating knowledge, for the stream began at ground level, up a support post, then took a right angle turn onto the roof beam and so along to the food. I had to grease the upright beam at the base to stop the flow of ants. Always when ants or bees find anything sweet and edible, there is a mass onslaught within next to no time. Probably it is some sort of mental telepathy that they use.

Captain Bullied had warned me about the risk of an ant invasion, even by leaving a few crumbs around after a meal, so I was scrupulous to sweep the place clean — until one day, when it was ideal for burning off the stubble, I loaded a couple of bundles of hessian, paraffin, a wire drag and a besom into the truck and went immediately after dinner to get the job done. It was a half mile journey through dense bush and after manoeuvering carefully along the narrow sandy track, eventually I emerged on to the open wheat field where a slight breeze made it ideal to keep the burn between the fire breaks and I had the besom handy in case of any wayward flames. The straw was tinder dry in the hot afternoon sun. I fastened some paraffin-soaked hessian to the wire drag, set it alight, then started dragging the flaming cloth along the inside of the fire break. As the long straw caught alight, I started running because the acreage was large and I wanted it burnt out by nightfall.

Suddenly, for no apparent reason, a couple of 'willie-willies' (small whirlwinds) sprang up, tossing the flames about and whirling sparks high into the air. Then the wind increased and changed direction and heavy thunder clouds rolled overhead. I was in trouble — real trouble! Once fire starts in the dry bush, there is no stopping it. Sparks and lighted pieces of straw sailed over my head and within seconds the ominous crackle of fire in the dry undergrowth could be heard. As I raced back for the truck, sheets of flame shot into the air, followed by explosions as more areas caught alight. I revved up the engine, slammed the clutch in and was off back along the track, enveloped in swirling clouds of smoke and sparks. Why the truck didn't turn over was a miracle, for quite a few times it tipped at an alarming angle as I swung around the sharp bends, with wheels skidding in the sandy ruts, but with the roar of flames racing along behind, there was no alternative. I was also worried that the petrol tank might explode in the searing heat. However, when I was halfway back, my guardian angel must have wakened up, for there was a sudden crash of thunder overhead and the rain started coming down in torrents. The downpour quelled the fire as quickly as it had started.

When I got back, I parked the truck, rolled a cigarette and sat smoking quietly to calm my frayed nerves before going over to the house. House doors in the bush are seldom closed. For one reason, there is no one around to trespass and open doors allow free passage of cooling draughts. Approaching the veranda, I noticed an unusual number of ants running around and, mounting the steps, I saw to my alarm and dismay that the whole place was swarming with black ants. Floor, table, chairs, everything was covered and seemed alive with the active, pugnacious insects. I had forgotten to sweep up and clear the table before I left and this was the result. Getting a broom, I swept thousands of them out of doors, but they kept pouring in through cracks in the floor boards, doors and windows. From the water tank by the back door, I filled bucket after bucket of water and tried to flood them out, but as fast as I swept and flooded, further battalions came in. It just wasn't my day! In the end, realising the futility of my present method, I sized up the situation. Oil and only oil would hold them at bay. So, grabbing a bucket, I filled it from a fifty gallon drum of oil in the garage and finding four columns of ants making their way to the bungalow from different directions, I poured oil across their paths and the assault stopped immediately. It took two days to clear them out and they smelt abominably. In fact they are known in the bush as 'piss ants' and they couldn't have a more appropriate name. The smell reminded me of when, as boy scouts, we used to urinate on the camp fire to put it out.

Ants will fight fire even to their death. The ant hills were often but a few yards apart and had to be cleared from land to be cultivated. To burn them down we used to knock the tops off then set them alight with a few burning embers. Slowly they smouldered away to ground level and all the time a valiant but hopeless fight was waged against it by the ants. Some rushed around, frantically waving their antenna at the glowing mass, while others ran to and fro, humping oval eggs as big as themselves. Frequently, a bush fire only left them scorched, for the outer crust had to be broken to set them alight.

Another interesting phenomenon was the migration of caterpillars. A column of them about a yard long would wend their way slowly along the ground, head to tail. If the last caterpillar was gently taken away, the whole column stopped. If it wasn't replaced, they would wait twenty minutes before slowly moving on again. It is obvious that many lower forms of life have a communal awareness as well as an individual self-preservation consciousness, for this instinct is not only apparent in the ants and caterpillars, but in flocks of birds and shoals of fresh water bream and pilchards in the clear water below.

A shoal of a hundred or so fry would shimmer like silver in the sunlit water, then simultaneously dart left or right. Each movement and change of direction was automatic, as though one awareness governed the lot. Each batch of spawn, on coming to life, apparently forms its own shoal, for all the fish in each shoal were similar in size and they swam as a unit. We fished with three or four hooks on a line and the massacre was terrible. As soon as the baited hooks were thrown in, a shoal of small fry raced for them and as these were not wanted, the line was hastily withdrawn again. Maimed and torn fry with blood oozing from lacerations made by the hooks, flopped about on the surface of the water. One minute they had been living in a sunlit, joyous paradise, the next they were flopping about in a painful hell. It is amazing the strength of fish in the water. If two were caught at the same time on one line, it took much strength to drag them through the water and yet they may have been but nine or ten inches long. Even one small fish felt like a conger eel.

Fishing is cruel. Even then, I knew it to be cruel. At first, threading a live worm on the fish hook was distasteful, but by hardening any finer feelings or squeamishness and by repetition, I soon became hardened to it. Then, to hook a fish in the mouth became, by habit, a pleasant pastime. Fishermen in competition often catch fish, pull the hook from the lacerated gullet, then after weighing them, throw them back into the river or lake for further 'sport'. All these cases of cruelty perpetrated by man, including fishing, fox hunting, hare, badger and stag hunting and the shooting of 'game' are degrading. The argument put forward by the killers is that all nature is red in tooth and claw. Their logic is that anything animals do is right for humans to do likewise. Yet if we behaved in public view the way animals do at times, we would be locked up — and quite rightly so. So only the activities of the carnivorous predators that suit the killer and merciless hunter are extolled as being natural by this backward section of humankind. Then again, to say that all nature is red in tooth and claw is erroneous, for herbivores far outnumber carnivores and lead a life much more in keeping with spiritual ethics than many people. Although we are undoubtedly superior in brain power, that very superiority is often used for the negation of the higher ideals. Man mistakes reflected light from the depths — tainted with elemental forces of materialism, of bloodshed, of disease and darkness — as the true light, and so long as he lives as a predator and is motivated by his lower nature, so will he be in bondage to that animal level, and all the religious teachings in the world will be powerless to alter that fact.

There is no doubt that different foods dictate the behaviour of the eater, for although the effect may appear unrelated to the cause, it is relevant to compare the peaceful nature of the vegetarian and fruit eating animals such as the anthropoids, to the aggressive nature of the carnivores. Although we like to prove that we are 'civilised' by killing our victims instantly, the primordial, uncivilised instinct to kill remains, and we see the result in acts of war, murder, vandalism and other forms of barbarism.

Dog has her day

I must return to where I left off, at the Captain's place, but bear in mind, dear reader, that as I relate this narrative, I was still in darkness and unaware of the unity of life.

Dog was really the most intelligent animal I have ever met, for she had the unusual ability of being able to follow the line of a pointing finger and to recognise the target — a most unusual perception in any animal. Sometimes the fowl would mill around together, turkeys and hens in one moving mass, yet Dog could single one out and hold it down with her open mouth until I picked it up, nor did she injure the bird. If I pointed to a turkey that appeared to be in need of oil treatment, Dog would rear up onto her hind legs to get a better view of the flock and keep looking at my pointing finger to single out the bird. Once she had made sure which one was to be caught, away she would go and quite gently, but firmly, hold it down. I have never met such ability in a dog before, or since.

She loved going out with me on hunting expeditions. When I picked up the gun and sallied forth into the surrounding woods, her excitement knew no bounds. I never used a spray-shot gun, for that type of firearm doesn't give the game a fair chance. A single-shot gun gives the user an unfair advantage in any case, but to use a spray-shot is much more cruel, for it is more likely to injure without killing and needs no expertise or skill on the part of the hunter — any mutt can cause havoc with that firearm. So away I would go with my 'point two two' with Dog running in wild and delighted sorties around me. There was only one flaw in Dog's logic while on these excursions and that was on the point of ownership of the quarry. If I was successful and shot a bird on the wing, Dog would catch it in her mouth before it reached the ground, obediently bring it back to me, but then would not part with it! She would stand facing me with bowed head, holding the dead bird in her mouth. 'Put it down!' I commanded in a strict voice, but such a demand fell on deaf ears. 'Dog. Put it down. Drop it!' but she would just stand motionless while the rights of ownership were battled out. I knew what she was thinking. She had caught it, not me, so why should I have it? In the end I would say, 'Go on then. Eat it,' and in a matter of only seconds only the tail remained of the kill.

Once we were walking along a track with Dog at heel, when a kangaroo broke cover about fifty yards ahead. Dog immediately gave chase and I could hear by the thumping of the tail that Dog was bringing it back. I raised my rifle ready to take aim quickly and snap-shoot when it appeared. It is not easy to shoot a 'roo even under the best of conditions, for it must be shot in the head for the shot to be fatal and as this one was quite small, the aim had to be accurate. This one could be across the track and back into safety of the bush in one hop. My judgement that it would break cover about thirty yards ahead, wasn't far out. I fired, but missed. Dog raced after it through the bush in a half circle and rounded it back for me to have another shot. I fired when it broke cover, and missed again. Dog followed in hot pursuit and turned it yet again to break cover. As it took its third leap across the track, I fired, and missed yet again! Dog came racing out of the bush about ten yards behind, dropped flat on her stomach, panting for breath and looked at me, as much as to say, 'I give up!' It was 'face losing' for me, because she thought I was infallible and to miss three times was, to put it mildly, bewildering to her, but I had to laugh at her incredulous look of astonishment.

The first time we went out, I took sandwiches and a flask of coffee to have a little refreshment during the midday heat, but I soon found that any interlude like this was impossible. In the heat of early afternoon, while Dog was ahead looking for quarry, I found an open space. The area was covered in a profusion of blue and orange donkey orchids and the still air was heavy with scent from the golden wattle. The leaves on the trees hung limp in the heat while a lone cockatoo sat preening itself on a nearby eucalyptus. Although it was red and white it was quite hard to see amid the sun-dappled leaves. I leant my rifle against a redgum and had just sat at the bole, when something jumped onto my leg. It was a scorpion! I've never acted faster in my life and with three or four flicks of the hand kept it moving to prevent it stinging me. Its last jump was over my head. Its action was like a short spring giving a lash as it winds and unwinds. The reason why a scorpion looks like a jumping spring is because the tail is brought over the head to sting in one continuous and rapid motion. Their sting is venomous and they are so vicious that if trapped in a box they will sting themselves to death.

Not wanting to test providence, I moved to the bole of another tree and sitting down, took sandwiches and the coffee flask from my haversack. The cockatoo had stopped its preening and now watched my antics with head held sideways and red crest raised in a gesture of surprise. I had just taken a bite from a sandwich, when Dog emerged from the dense bush. She stopped dead at the sight of me sitting. From her attitude it was obvious what was running through her mind. 'How dare you sit and waste time while all this excitement is going on!' For Dog never tired. She bounded with energy from dawn till dusk and with her new-found freedom of hunting with me, every moment was to be savoured and utilised to the full. She looked in consternation for a second or two, then raced up with her face a couple of inches off mine and created pandemonium in the silent forest by barking continuously. 'Get up! Get up! Get up!' I tempted her with half a sandwich. She jumped back a foot. 'Don't you dare soft-soap me!' I tried to carry on eating, but it was impossible. She just would not approve of such time wasting. The bush life had wakened up with the din. A laughing jackass was having a hearty, vulgar laugh at my expense as it flew over-head. The cockatoo had started screeching and the green parrots with yellow-ringed necks called 'twenty-eights' were squawking from the surrounding trees in resentment at the dog's noisy presence. I returned the food and flask to the haversack with a sigh of resignation and when I stood up and grasped the rifle, Dog bounded around in delight, then she was off again to scout ahead to try to raise some game. As I left the small clearing, it became quiet again. I looked up into the branches of the eucalyptus as I passed, the cockatoo was still watching with raised crest, but suddenly the silence was shattered again by the laughing jackass sending its raucous laughter echoing through the bush.

Cockatoos are very wise and interesting. One year, Joe and I got a harvesting job with an Australian family who had a tame cockatoo. One of its wings had been clipped so that it couldn't fly. On a Sunday morning, when everyone wanted an extra hour's lie in, the parrot would have none of it and would sit on the veranda rail, shouting continually 'Marge! Marge! Marge!' — that was the name of the farmer's wife. His daughter Evonne was thirteen and a bit of a tomboy. She used to chase the bird as it ran along the ground. When she drew near, it would stop running, sink down in a crouching position and quite plainly say, 'Ah, poor Vonnie! Ah, poor Vonnie!' obviously currying favour for gentle treatment. So who can say that birds have no brains?

I am not in favour of mushy sentimentality towards lower forms of life. Show kindness and allow them to lead their own lives to the full, but do not pamper or make fools of them as do some pet lovers. These people are really thinking of the comfort and protection which they may receive from the animal and although they will hotly contend that it loves them in return, this is not the reason to justify ownership. An animal can never be 'civilised' for it has neither the brain capacity not the logic to be one with society. Life, other than our own, is governed by temperament, emotion and instinct and many serious attacks have occurred through assuming they have an intellect equal to our own. A well fed animal is naturally passive and content, but give your hungry dog a meaty bone, then try to take it away and your 'wouldn't hurt a fly' pet will mutilate your hand with a savage bite. Herbivores are totally different. Take the food from the mouth of a herbivore and it will just stop chewing. Return the food and the chewing starts again. I know this to be true because I have tried it.

About cats

Cats, I think, are the most amenable to human company and environment, for a cat remains a separate unit in spite of all the endearments and civilised comforts bestowed upon it. As everyone knows, they maintain their independence and will only react to your wishes if it suits them. I do believe that if a domesticated cat has comfort and freedom to roam, it is contented, yet surprisingly, wild cats are the most vicious animals to encounter. Once in the bush Harry Oldfield and I found a nest of seven wild kittens in a deserted shack. The mother was probably out hunting. They milled about together on what remained of a rag mat in the corner of a dark room and evidently were but a few days old, for their eyes had only just opened. They were tiny bundles of playful tortoiseshell fur, yet when we picked them up, they immediately became vicious, spitting, little fluffy balls of fury. They rolled onto their backs in the open palms of our hands and with legs raised and claws out ready to scratch, spat at us with venom all the time. Small and attractive as they were, there was something rather frightening about their viciousness. All the cat family are clean, self-reliant creatures and this family includes the tiger, leopard, puma, cheetah and lynx. When one of these animals stops cleaning itself, it is a sure sign of approaching death. Sometimes they have been trapped by the simple expedient of putting a sticky substance on their tail. They become so intent on the task of trying to lick their paws clean that the hunters have been able to get close enough to trap them in a net.

I once had a beautiful tortoiseshell cat called Peta. She was a real spitfire! At that time, near my cottage, there was a small paddock of long grass and she loved to play hide-and-seek there, with me on all fours as part of the game. Being higher than her, I could see the tall grass moving where she was stealthily creeping around and when we met (by a bit of manoeuvering) face to face, she would take a flying leap into the air with excitement and be off again for another spell of tracking. In one part of the paddock there was an old decayed stump of a tree, with a patch of bare ground and this was Peta's neutral area. If she was there when I emerged from the surrounding cover, she would take not the slightest notice of my presence, but calmly carry on grooming herself while I waited patiently; then she would take a sudden jump into the jungle and the game would be on again.

Now cats will never deign to show any particular interest in humans — apart from meal times of course — and Peta was no exception. Sometimes in the long summer evenings, I would come in tired from work and have known by a sort of mental telepathy that Peta wanted another game in the paddock. The prospect of crawling on hands and knees for an hour or so for her amusement didn't always appeal, but Peta had her own method of persuasion. As I carried her plate of food out to the stone flagged porch, she would follow but ignore the proffered meal and pass straight out through the open door, then sit about five yards away cleaning herself. 'Come on, Peta,' I would say, picking the plate up and holding it out, but she was too much engrossed in meticulously licking a paw clean. I would go out to pick her up, but when I got near she would run another few yards and resume her toilet and always the direction of her short runs was towards the long grass. Invariably, in the end she had her own way. 'Come on then, Peta,' I would say, going past her and on to the paddock. Immediately her grooming and meticulous licking of paws was forgotten and she would race ahead, with tail erect, take a flying leap into her playground and another session of hide-and-seek began.

Even as a kitten, Peta liked to hang by her front paws and swing on any convenient bar; a very unusual pastime for any ordinary cat, but then Peta wasn't ordinary. I had a clothes horse in the bedroom and sometimes at dawn I awoke to find her swinging gently from the lower rail. This amusement was harmless enough but one evening, while I was distempering the living room, she lost her grip and fell into the bucket of distemper. The steps that led from the living room to the upstairs bedrooms, had no back to the treads and I'd placed the bucket of distemper behind the steps while doing the wall at the side. Unnoticed by me, she must have resorted to her usual pastime of swinging from the back of a step and slipped off, for suddenly there was a 'plop' and, looking around, I beheld Peta, startle eyed, with only her head above the distemper. 'Peta!' I shouted in annoyance. Before I could do anything, she jumped out of the bucket and ran from the room, blazing a trail of bright yellow distemper along the stone flagged floor as she went. I ran after her into the passage — and there she was, with her head stuck inside a small cardboard box, hoping like an ostrich that she was hidden! 'All right, Peta,' I said in a reassuring voice, and picking her up I took her to the scullery where, under a slow running tap, I gradually washed the distemper from her long fur. Luckily it was water soluble. Cats don't like water, but Peta was quite submissive to the treatment, although I noticed at times she gave me a quick look to make sure that I was still in a good mood after the accident.

Later, while I cleared up the floor, Peta, sitting on a chair after the towelling, groomed herself and so far as she was concerned, everything was back to normal. I don't think her logic extended to the fact that I, on hands and knees, continually swilling and mopping the floor had any connection with her escapade.

A man and his wife, both pet lovers, lived in a cottage about half a mile away and I had the bright idea of taking Peta there. They kept some ten dogs and fifteen cats. All the man's wages must have gone to feeding them. Anyway, on an evening visit, I took Peta with me thinking that she would enjoy the company of her own species, but nothing could have been further from her wishes. She just sat all the evening on one of the chairs with legs folded beneath her, looking the picture of misery. I think she was embarrassed too. She took not the slightest notice of the other cats and if one reached up and tried to touch noses in a friendly gesture, she turned her head away in utter disdain. She just wasn't interested in this riff-raff! The funny part about it was that in her own house she was a real ray of sunshine and would play with anything. As I carried her back, she reached up a couple of times to touch my nose. I knew that she was telling me, 'Thank goodness we've left that place.'

It is always a mistake to hurt an animal in trying to 'teach it a lesson'. Every animal accepts a human as a superior and once it knows what you want, it will always comply. Should you hit an animal to hurt it, it reacts in two ways. First, it is no longer your friend and second, it becomes so frightened that its one object is to get away and, being terrified, it doesn't connect the chastisement with the misdeed. Give any animal a tap or two and a stern word and once it knows why, it will comply with your wishes, but to hit an animal hard 'to teach it a lesson' just does not work. When I was a child we gave a kitten to a woman visitor. Later on, I remember asking how it was getting on. 'Aye,' she replied, speaking to my mother, 'I've belted hell out of that cat and still it's not house trained.' Poor kitten. No wonder. Had it happened now, I would have demanded the cat back from the woman, but at that time I passively accepted cruelty as part of life.

The Captain's return

I have digressed and must return to the Australian farm. The Captain was due back at any time and as he was the type of man that anyone would be rather 'for' than 'against', I put Dog back on the run wire and resumed her diet of raw eggs and bran, for he was strict about her menu. As arranged, I had left the car near the siding ready for the Captain's return and got a lift back from the storekeeper with a supply of rations.

One evening as darkness was setting in, Dog started barking. I went out to investigate. Alternately she looked at me and then down the track. I guessed it was the Captain returning. After waiting a while in the cool, welcome evening breeze, I got an occasional glimpse of a car's headlights as it manoeuvered up the winding track and soon it appeared into the clearing.

'Have a good time, Captain?' I asked, as he got out of the car.

'Geordie,' he replied, breaking into one of his rare smiles, 'I've spent nearly the whole time in Freemantle, watching the shipping. Met one of the Captains from the P & O liners. Went to a sailing regatta on the Swan and all in all had a right royal time.' He didn't mention women, but as he radiated a kindly nature, allied to a stern but smart appearance, I imagine that he enjoyed his 'fair' share. Dog gave him a 'right royal' welcome too when he went over to her. That is one thing about dogs, they display joy and affection in no uncertain manner and Dog showed all these emotions, in spite of his keeping her on a restricted run.

In the bungalow, everything had been scrubbed and dusted and anything that could be spit-polished had been spit-polished ready for his return and although he didn't comment, I don't think it went unnoticed.

'Any visitors while I've been away?'

'Only one, a swaggie. I gave him a meal and some rations and told him a white lie — that Dog roamed free all night.'

'Fair enough. You don't want them hanging around. Now knock up a meal, Geordie, while I feed the dog and bring in the luggage.'

'Right, Captain!' After the repast, while the Captain sat contentedly smoking his pipe in the warm glow from the two hurricane lamps on the table, I told him various bits of information. I recounted about the sudden change of wind during the burning of the paddock, but I omitted to mention that his new truck nearly tipped over. I mentioned how the poultry had fared; how two turkeys had been lost — one killed by the eagle hawk and another had died in spite of the olive oil treatment.

The Captain had no saddle hacks, so next day we wended our way through the narrow track in the car to see the paddock. All the straw had been burned — plus four hundred acres of bush! The firebreak at the far end of the paddock had been effective, if that was any consolation. Back at the house, both the tractor and header had been cleaned and greased and a good supply of logs had been stacked in an old five hundred gallon water tank lying on its side. From the absence of any criticism, I gathered that he was quite satisfied with my caretaking. That night, we slept on a couple of trestle beds, one at each end of the veranda, and I had just got comfortable when in the darkness, the Captain barked out in his sternest mid-Atlantic voice, 'Geordie!'

I leapt out of bed and stood to attention in my shirt tails, 'Yes, Captain?'

'What did you feed Dog on while I was away?'

'Raw egg and bran.'

'She didn't have any game, did she?'

'No Captain, no game!'

'That's good. I don't want her to have game, in case she turns on the poultry.'

'Yes. That is a risk.'

'Goodnight, Geordie.'

'Night, Captain.' I crawled back into bed. She'd eaten game every day but I couldn't imagine Dog, with her intelligence, getting the two mixed up.

Next morning, after washing and shaving in the cool of the veranda, the Captain went indoors to prepare the breakfast, while I went to feed the dog and bring the car round for our trip to the siding. I had just fetched the car and was getting out near the veranda steps, when the Captain came out. He looked distressed — unusual for him for he rarely showed any emotion.

Perhaps a favourite aunt had died or something, because he had been reading some mail brought back from the siding.

'Anything wrong, Captain?' I asked with some concern.

'Geordie, Geordie,' he said in the voice of a broken man. 'You've mixed the lard with the dripping!'

I'd fallen off my pedestal.

The journey back

Soon after this, Joe and I set sail for England in the *Jervis Bay*. She was a lovely sleek ship that had been converted to a cruiser during the 1914-18 war. Narrow beamed and fast, she gave us a great voyage home. The atmosphere too was more relaxed than on the outward journey, for on the way out to Australia there had been a feeling of tension and apprehension, as no one knew what the new country held in store for them. Now, all the passengers were carefree and friendly. Games and festivities went with a swing. There were deck quoits, obstacle races, acrobatic teams performing and of course, sun bathing and in the evenings concerts, dances and community singing.

Yet, as we passed through the 'Bay' and approached the colder northern climate, this relaxation gradually changed. Groups kept more to themselves and as we entered the Channel everyone had reverted to their class-conscious, formal selves. Gone was the free and easy chatting to 'travel companions' and the 'join our tea party' invitations. Now, passengers walked muffled up around the promenade decks in two's and three's, having their constitutional, and now only the vicar on board was inundated with invitations to afternoon tea. I am sure that climate has a lot to do with attitude.

Joe's father met us at Southampton and I stayed on board until we docked at Hull. The last I heard of Joe, for we didn't keep up a correspondence, was that he was employed as a life-guard in one of the Welsh coast resorts.

LIFE IN CORNWALL

T HE COTTAGE APPEALED to me on first sight. This was the place I was looking for: thick stone walls leaning at such crazy angles that made one wonder how on earth they defied the law of gravity, yet looking so rock-like and secure. Thatched roof above whitewashed walls added a smugness to security and, set half a mile from the nearest habitation, promised peace and tranquillity. By using a hand pump above the sink in the kitchen, water was drawn from a well in the centre of the long, narrow garden. I decided, there and then, to rent it from the London owner. At the Cornish farm-cum-store-cum-post office, I handed back the keys to Mrs Elton, the middle-aged farmer's wife who ran the shop, and told her that I had decided to rent the cottage and would be her new neighbour.

Her eyes opened wide, 'And live there — alone?'

'Yes. Why not?' She gave an involuntary shudder.

'I'm going to keep poultry,' I informed her, 'and do some gardening. I'll be moving in next week end.'

As she took the keys, her face broke into a smile that could be interpreted in two ways; that I was either a hero, or just plain daft. 'If you are interested,' she said, seeming to relax a little as though she rather liked the idea of me moving in, 'I have a white Whyandotte hen sitting on a dozen eggs. They should be hatched in a few days, if you want them.'

'Right, Mrs Elton, thanks. I'll remember that.' As I left the store, she gave me another smile. This time it was warmer but still incredulous.

The cottage smelt damp and fusty when I arrived in the late afternoon of the following week end, so I decided to sleep on the couch in the sitting room, with a good fire ablaze in the open hearth. A nearby thicket provided ample dry wood and in next to no time I had a fire burning merrily with an armful of short, thick branches at the side to keep it going. I had another look around my new abode. All the ground floor was stone flagged and the furnishings were sparse but adequate. In the living room was a deal table, four wooden chairs, a small Dutch dresser with half a dozen cups hanging from hooks and in the two drawers and cupboard was a good supply of crockery and cutlery. The only floor covering was a multi-coloured rag mat in front of the open fireplace. One side of the room had been partitioned off to provide a narrow kitchen. In this there was a stone sink, water pump and a calor gas cooker. From some water left in a brown jug in the sink, I primed the pump, then vigorously worked the handle up and down, hoping for results. Brown, brackish water started to gulp out and one or two black things fell into the sink. I peered down in the dim light — they were black slugs. Certainly the brew I made from this water supply was going to have 'body' if nothing else!

The sitting room had the inevitable horse-hair sofa, on which I decided to sleep until the place had dried out. The only other furniture in this room, were three old arm chairs and another rag mat in front of the open hearth. A few bumble bees droned near the lattice window as the last rays of the setting sun slanted in. The cottage faced nearly due north and I noticed later that this was the only time any sunlight got around to the front, and that was only in high summer. There were two bedrooms upstairs, both with deep stone settings around small dormer windows and from which the light was partly concealed by the overhanging thatch. In one room was a double bed with a stout rope tied from the bed head to a hook in the stone wall. The castors on the legs were tight up against the wall, while the top, where the rope was attached, was a good foot away. Whether the bed was supporting the wall, or the other way about, I didn't try to find out in case of calamity. In a corner, a triangular table covered with green baize held a chipped, green and white water jug and basin and on a mahogany chest of drawers stood a framed mirror with a piece of glass missing. In the other room, across the landing, were two single beds and a dressing table.

Another feature that added novelty to the cottage was that the floor boards were all different lengths and shapes. Some parts of the floor sloped up and some parts down and nearly every board creaked ominously when stood upon. On the single beds, the bedding had been folded and placed on the mattresses, so I took two blankets to use on the sofa, but before going downstairs, stood at one of the windows, admiring the view. About half a mile away, between the fold of two hills, could be seen a triangle of blue sea, and in the crystal clear air, seagulls whirled and called their plaintive cries overhead. It was certainly a poet or a painter's paradise, far from madding crowds.

Bumps in the night

Taking only my jacket and shoes off and with the blankets over me, I was soon ensconced and comfortable on the sofa and although the place felt a bit spooky, the glow and flicker of the flames had a reassuring friendliness as the dark night set in. After the long journey and tiring day, I soon fell into a peaceful sleep, but could not have slept for long before I wakened again. The fire was still burning brightly, but I had a definite feeling that there was another presence in the room. I was right there was! For, looking across the floor, I saw a rat, slowly moving from the direction of my couch towards the door. It must have been blind, for as I watched by the light from the fire, when it got to the door, it gently bumped along the bottom until it found the centre slab that had been worn by a few generations of feet, then crawled through the gap.

An hour or so later, I was wakened again by a loud rumbling sound that at first I took to be thunder. The fire had now died down to a dull glow. As I listened, I realised that the noise came from the room above. It wasn't thunder, it was beds and furniture being pushed and swung around and the rumbling and squeaking of the castors became nearly deafening. It was either intruders who were unaware that the place was now occupied, passing the furniture through the windows (for there was no one coming down the stairs) or else all the poltergeists from the psychic world had joined forces for a heyday. There was only one thing to do — investigate.

Now surprise attack is always the best form of defence. So, quietly getting off the sofa and making my way to the door, I tried to lift the latch silently. Unfortunately it was a metal bar type. As the latch lifted it gave a slight metallic click. All the noise above stopped immediately. Everything went dead silent. I had the eerie feeling that all life in the dark cottage, both animate and ghostly, was not only aware of my presence, but eagerly awaited my next move. Now that silence was unnecessary I ran upstairs, unlatched the bedroom door and pushed it wide open with my foot, then striking a match and shielding the light from my eyes, ventured cautiously in. I expected to find everything in disorder and to catch a couple of robbers in the act, as the light from the match dimly lit the room, but no such scene revealed itself. I went into the centre of the room, lit another match and held it high. I just could not understand it. The furniture was in exactly the same place as it had been in the daylight, neither was there anyone there! This, to say the least, was baffling, for the commotion I had heard certainly had not been a figment of my imagination.

There was only one way to solve the mystery and that was to stay quietly in the dark room and await events. So I sat on one of the deep stone sills and very soon the mystery was solved. It was rats! The thatch was alive with them. There was a squeak or two above my head, then the pattering of paws, followed by rumbling sounds and louder squeaking as they seemed to be rolling about locked together in either play or combat. Soon it was the former bedlam again, for the panelled hardboard ceiling magnified the sound to an amazing degree. I sat for a while listening, then clapped my hands. Immediately, there was dead silence. They all froze where they were — listening. I knew instinctively that they were well aware of the new tenant and were probably wondering what I was like. However, now that the mystery was solved, there was no need to stay, so I went downstairs and, getting comfortable again on my couch, was soon in dreamland.

I must have slept for a couple of hours, when I wakened again. It wasn't any suspicious noise that disturbed my sleep this time, but the opposite — the utter silence and blackness. The fire had gone out completely and the blackness was so black and the silence so intense that I really wondered if I had departed from this world. I coughed self-consciously and heard the sound echoing across the desolate fields outside. Anyway, I felt reassured, because a corpse cannot cough, so I went to sleep. In my sleep I became aware of tapping sounds and suddenly sat bolt upright. Just outside the sitting room door, someone was tapping a metal-tipped walking stick on the stone flags. I wondered how an intruder had got in, for both the front and back doors had been securely bolted. I listened to make sure it wasn't the atmosphere of the place playing tricks on my imagination. Tap, tap, tap — silence. The eerie tapping was real enough. 'Right, chum,' I thought, 'if you're trying to scare me with your spooky taps, I'll turn the tables on you.' For by now I was getting not frightened but irritated by all these nocturnal goings on.

Quietly getting off the sofa, I made my way towards the door intending to swing it open quickly and to swipe a fist into the dark passage, hoping to connect with either a simple minded cane-tapping local, or a Frankenstein, but half way to the door I was stopped dead in my tracks, for I had stepped into a pool of icy cold water in my stockinged feet. The tapping outside continued, but I also became aware that it was raining. Immediately I connected the two and, upon opening the door and striking a match, discovered that someone had placed a tin bucket on the floor to catch the rain drops that were building up on a lone hanging thatch straw and dripping into it. Three ominous drips at a time!

That cottage was always spooky and gave one the feeling that someone else was there. That is until eventually and involuntarily, I worked an act of exorcism by splitting a ghost in half!

Sometimes, when I had been washing in the narrow scullery after returning from work, I had felt compelled to go into the living room to reassure myself that it was empty. The rats alone seemed to be oblivious or immune to the psychic entities that hovered around. The rats kept to their territory and I to mine and they remained there, regardless. After the first night's escapade, they never disturbed my sleep again by cavorting on the ceiling. Only once did I have a bit of a shock and that was during the night when I sat up in bed to stroke what I thought was a cat and realised when I touched it that it was a rat, taking a short cut to the open window via the bedspread. My attitude towards them at first was 'There's a rat — kill it' for I was a victim of the accepted school of hate towards the species. At odd times I heard them running along behind the boxed skirting boards and put poison down to try to kill them off but later regretted it, for they never bothered me and a lot of these poisons kill by burning the insides of the creatures.

Rats are very clean too. When I was a schoolboy, a friend of mine had two tame rats and they were always grooming themselves. At first I was scared to touch them, but they were so good natured and friendly that fear soon gave way to affection. They would run up our arms and nestle against our necks, but if anyone was scared and timid they seemed to sense it and would not persist in any unwelcome action. How they can breed them in laboratories and then inflict untold cruelties in an effort to find remedies for diseases which, by the way, only correct diet will cure, beats me. Rats must be kept down. There is no doubt about that for they create a lot of damage and have been known to carry the plague. We must remember too that plagues spread in the middle ages when lack of hygiene and filth in the streets and homes fostered disease. Unfortunately, we still have filth in the streets from dogs fouling the pavements, yet if any disease was blamed upon dogs there would be an outcry from all the pet owners in the land at the mere suggestion that Fido or Rover were in any way to blame.

The cat takes over

'Would you like a cat?'

A servant girl, who worked for the local doctor, stood at the door of the cottage, holding a large, dark and light brown cat.

'The holiday people who owned it must have gone home and left it at the caravan site, because it was found around the doctor's house looking for food,' she explained. Now I'm sure that in some previous incarnation I have been a cat, for all the felines seem to recognise me as a long lost relative — and me them! This cat was no exception, for its hazel eyes surveyed me with no element of fear or surprise. I put the back of my hand near his nose for him to get the radiation and immediately the friendship was sealed. The liking was mutual — as usual.

'Yes, I would love a cat,' I assured her and taking Charlie (for that's the name I gave him) from her arms, I carried him into the living room which he immediately began to explore and when that initial task was finished, looked somberly at me. The question conveyed by his eyes was obvious, 'How about some milk?' I jumped to it, gave him a saucerful and when he got busy lapping that up, I jumped on my scooter and went post-haste to Mrs Elton's for a few tins of cat food. When I got back, Charlie was sitting on my chair licking himself methodically, but he jumped down and followed me into the scullery. By some strange mental telepathy he seemed to know the reason for my errand. He sat, waiting patiently as I opened a tin and spooned half the contents onto a plate. When it was put on the stone flag, he sniffed to make sure it was the right brand, then without undue haste, commenced to consume the offering.

To sit in comfort in the evenings, I had brought an armchair into the living room, but Charlie soon put paid to that idea. After finishing his meal, he surveyed the armchair again, decided it would do, sat in the centre of the cushion and resumed his grooming. I drew up a wooden seat and sat opposite. The boss had arrived! Now that I had acquired a cat, my thoughts turned to the rats. How would they fare together? I knew they would, even now, be aware of the intruder and probably holding a council of war about their next move, but as it turned out everything went smoothly. I am pretty sure that some left in utter disgust at my inconsideration, but the dozen or so that remained became part of the trinity. They lived their lives, Charlie his, and I mine. The rats lived mainly upstairs, Charlie and I downstairs and none interfered with the other's life-style.

Later, as darkness set in, I was sitting on the wooden chair reading, when I noticed that Charlie was becoming restless. He started to pace beside the door and window, wanting to get out, but I didn't want him to go out on the first night because he might get lost. He came up to me, miaowed a couple of times, then returned to the door. After I lit the lamp and the evening wore on, he grew more agitated. The lamplight did nothing to pacify him. 'No, Charlie,' I said, stroking him. 'Tomorrow. But not tonight.' He sat looking at me with luminous eyes, then went back to the door, in dumb appeal to be let out. Shortly after ten o'clock, I put more milk down, gave him a reassuring stroke or two, then went upstairs to bed. Just when I was getting comfortable, I heard the cat miaowing louder and 'bumping' sounds. I went down to investigate and actually found my new friend trying to break a glass window pane in his frenzy to escape. Immediately I opened the front door, he shot out as if the place were — well — haunted! It was a pity that he left, for by the speedy nature of his exit, it was very doubtful whether he would return. I could only hope.

The bedroom window was always open through the night and the over-hanging thatch hung so low that the sash had to be pushed hard to open. Between the bedroom windows, it valleyed down to cover the front porch and you could stand outside the door at the front of the cottage and quite easily touch the roof. Next morning at daybreak, there was a rustling in the thatch. I didn't take much notice as I thought it was one of the rats returning home, but this was followed by a 'thump' on the floor and lo and behold, Charlie had entered the bedroom! He seemed as pleased to get back as he had been eager to leave the night before and, jumping onto the bed beside me, purred like a dynamo while I stroked him, yet his determination to get out of the cottage as darkness set in always remained.

The only break to this rule was when he returned at times through the night carrying a baby rabbit which he deposited on my bed. This love offering wasn't particularly welcome, for it meant getting out of a warm bed, putting on wellies, gently grasping the furry bunny with a towel and taking it back into the field. I never touched them by hand, because wild creatures are often rejected by their own species if they have been handled by a human. There wasn't always a good sequel to these midnight visits, for sometimes I saw Charlie silhouetted against the window, carrying a small bunny by the back of the neck as he jumped into the room. I squirmed in the darkness while he crushed the skull and crunched away as he ate the bones. Next morning there was only the small rear entrail left. Fur, bones and everything else had disappeared. I think his offerings to me, placed on my pillow, were meant for my supper.

Keeping hens

She had twelve yellow chicks when I brought her from Mr Elton's farm next to the multi-purpose store. She was a white Wyandotte and I carried her and the chicks in a strong cardboard box down the road to my cottage; and so I started my intriguing insight into the, so called, small mentality of hens. I realised eventually that if you have a spark of compassion, then the crime of causing suffering to even one of them will build up into its true proportion as a heinous sin. I could fill a book with my many experiences with hens that revealed a much larger brain and emotive capacity than the much abused species is ever given credit for. Of course this attitude could be ridiculed by a trader in battery hens, for anything taken from its natural environment can create a distorted picture; just as quoting a sentence out of context from a book can create an apparent contradiction to the general theme. My hens, without doubt, recognised the engine sound of my approaching scooter and would race helter-skelter down the inside of the hedge bordering the garden, trying to keep level with me when I returned home. If the engine wasn't cut off, because I was going on to the shop first, they would realise I wasn't stopping and come to an abrupt halt. Giving a quick backward glance, I saw them all looking in obvious dismay, as much as to say, 'Where on earth is he off to now!' Believe it or not, hens have feelings for one another as well, as I will prove later.

Anyway, to return to my purchase. I installed them in the garden shed on a Friday morning with mixed feelings of pride and trepidation because Charlie, my cat, might think the chicks were birds and promptly eat them. I had to take precautions. Now Charlie, as I mentioned before, had a lovely quiet nature but he was a marvellous hunter too, for he could catch birds on the wing. Sometimes, while washing and shaving in the early morning, I have watched him through the open window doing acrobatic feats with amazing speed and skill. He would sit by the roadside hedge, looking the picture of innocence, when suddenly he would crouch as a flock of sparrows approached. If they swooped low, intending to settle, Charlie would take a flying leap and swipe at one with his paw. Now I couldn't blame him for this mean behaviour because, living like the rest of us on a fallen planet, he was only doing what came naturally, but it highlights my concern for the chicks.

Next day, on the Saturday morning, Charlie was having a snooze by the kitchen fire with legs folded under him, nose nearly touching the rag mat. He was happy in dreamland. I seized the opportune moment, went out into the garden and opened the shed door. Mother hen majestically led out her chicks. Their excitement knew no bounds. As they milled around, odd ones took a daring excursion about a yard away, then raced back to the protection of the hen and the chorus of cheep, cheep, cheeping filled the air. Obviously they were none the worse for their confinement, neither were they bothered about the new surroundings. It was like watching perpetual motion; running little balls of yellow, all bursting with movement, life and joy.

Eventually, I went back into the cottage and started reading with one eye on the book and the other on Charlie. Soon the Wyandotte with her family followed me in, through the open back door. Cheep, cheep, cheep. Cheep, cheep, cheep. The little chicks were soon running all around the kitchen. I stopped reading and knelt down beside Charlie to make sure there was no slip-up. One ran between us and touched the cat's nose as it passed.

Charlie's eyes opened as he dreamily watched the retreating chick. Suddenly the little ball of yellow did a swivel turn and started to come back. Cheep, cheep. Cheep, cheep. Charlie's eyes opened wide and turned luminous as it approached. This wasn't a dream. This was for real! Cheep, cheep, cheep. As it brushed past his nose, Charlie turned cross-eyed trying to keep it in focus, then slowly sat up and raised a paw with all claws out. He was going to flatten it once and forever. Firmly I grasped the menacing paw. 'No, Charlie. No!' then gently patted his head to distract his attention. I felt him relax a little but his blazing, incredulous eyes were still on the chick. He tensed up again. I gently patted and stroked him again, then gently pushed him down. Suddenly, I could tell he had got the message, 'These birds are not for eating,' for he completely relaxed and resumed his interrupted sleep.

After that, they could run over him, which they did at times, but he would take not the slightest notice. I've always noticed that once animals know your wishes they will comply, not because they have to, but because they want to. Charlie never liked poultry, they were too noisy and too fussy for his quiet nature. Later on, I acquired eighty brown leghorns and to Charlie, they were just an unavoidable nuisance that had to be tolerated.

Now the first insight I had into the brain capacity of hens came soon after the chicks arrived. For one thing, I noticed that whenever there were visitors to the cottage, the Wyandotte invariably paraded her brood before admirers. Showing how, when she clucked and scratched the ground, all the chicks ran to her and did the same. Now you may think that this was just a natural instinct, but the second thing that happened, I could hardly believe at first, but it was true enough, and far more connected with mutual feeling than with instinct.

When I first got the chicks, one (it turned out to be a cockerel) had a foot barely attached by a fine thread of skin to the leg. The farmer's wife didn't know what had caused it but, as it was beyond repair, I snipped off the skin and used thread to attach a small cotton pad to the end of its leg. The pad was always off by the next morning and I was scared to tie the thread too tightly in case the blood flow was stopped. I even used adhesive tape, but that was no more effective. In the end I had to give up trying and soon he grew a hard lump on the end of his leg, but he always limped along, avoiding stones and hard surfaces.

My poultry all seemed to be jet propelled. They had an insatiable love of life and a zest that had to be seen to be believed. If I went out of the back door and called them, it wasn't just a rush, it was a stampede!

Now here is one of the amazing things that I would never have given credit for, had I not seen it. If I went out and called them, the whole flock, as I mentioned, made a mad rush towards me. That is, I should say, the whole flock bar two. For hurrying up the garden, well in the rear, would be the lame cockerel dodging the stones and a pullet who always waited for him! She would run a few yards, then wait for him to catch up, run another few yards and wait again, while he desperately zig-zagged along looking for soft soil. If grain had been thrown down, when she got within ten yards or so of it, she would then make a mad dash for it, knowing that he could make his own way now. At first, I thought there must be some other reason for her coming in short runs, but there wasn't. She always waited for him. So if we think that hens are just stupid and devoid of any feeling of compassion, then we had better think again — and think right, this time!

Many of us have become so callous in our nature through a habitual disregard for any other forms of life than our own, that to give them any credit for intelligence and compassion never enters our heads. For instance, to put thousands of hens into battery cages from which they emerge as helpless freaks, cries out for justice and must have a disastrous boomerang effect on mankind. I could go on and on about my experiences with poultry. How when a farmer warned me that a fox was around, I had to take all the pullets in to share the cottage with me and about their life of perfect bliss sitting on the settee in my best room — but more about that later.

A night visitor

As I mentioned before, from the time when I arrived, I always had a feeling that someone else was in the cottage — a feeling of another presence. Being a bachelor, I am used to being on my own and not bothered about it, but in this place I always had a lurking suspicion that someone else was there. However, I put it down to the fact that, being such a lonely place, it was the unusual quietness giving me a 'spooky' feeling. It was September when I moved in and, a month or so later, I went to bed one night and, being a good sleeper, was soon off in dreamland. I wakened again at about eleven thirty with a premonition that something was going to happen. 'Don't be daft,' I thought, 'What could happen? Nothing's going to happen.' I'd been facing the wall, so turned over and promptly went to sleep again.

Half an hour later, at midnight, I wakened again and, looking across the room, beheld a very broad-shouldered man with a moustache, standing just inside the door and looking at me arrogantly, as much as to say, 'What are you doing here?' My immediate thought was, 'So there was someone else in the cottage!' His attitude annoyed me, because I was paying the rent, not him! I was out of the bed in a flash and attacked, meaning to throw him, but to my amazement, my hand went right through the ghost and bumped the wall behind him! On looking around by the light of the moon that was streaming in through a small side window, I could still clearly see the head and lower part of the body, but the body had disappeared at the place where I had gone through. The apparition had the appearance of thick, greyish-brown smoke as I watched. It didn't drift away. It just went thinner and thinner until there was nothing left. Cold shivers ran up and down my spine for, to say the least, it was eerie! I realised too that the room had gone extremely cold.

When the ghost had vanished, I got a torch and went all over the house to reassure myself that no one was in the house. Of course, I drew a blank. The place was absolutely deserted. There and then, I decided not to tell anyone of my experience because they would naturally think I was 'seeing things,' chasing ghosts through the middle of the night. The funny thing was that, after that experience, I never again had the feeling that someone else was in the place, though I did have other weird experiences.

The following spring, I worked for a poultry farmer. He hatched eggs by the thousand in huge incubators and sold the chicks. After each hatching, a young woman came to 'sex' the chicks. Cockerels, which weren't wanted, were dropped into thick paper bags that had been used for delivering hundredweights of poultry food. As each bag was filled with suffocating chicks, it was tied at the open end to the exhaust pipe of the farmer's car. The engine was started and left ticking over. In this way, the hapless young life went back into eternity. The pullets were reared to become egg-laying machines and eventually would emerge from their battery cages as freaks of nature.

Working with me was an old man, Cecil Osborne. 'By the way,' he said one morning during our tea break, 'I used to live near your cottage when I was a lad.' He puffed at his pipe of tobacco for a while, meditating. 'Cloaks Cottage, isn't it?'

'Yes, that's right, Cecil,' I replied.

'There's an espalier pear tree growing up the back wall,' he went on, 'They had to divert the ditch for that, it was swamping the roots. Yes, I know the cottage well,' he mused. 'By the way, have you seen Sammy Littlejohn?'

I thought he meant someone living in the neighbourhood.

'No. Who's he, Cecil?'

'Oh,' he went on, pausing to tap the ashes out of his pipe, 'he's been dead these many years!'

I immediately became interested. 'What's he like? Cecil'

'Oh, a very broadshouldered, arrogant man,' he reflected, 'very pompous looking, with a bushy 'tache'. He went on to describe in exact detail, the ghost I'd gone for! I didn't tell him of my experience and replied that I hadn't seen him.

'Oh, you'll be seeing him,' he replied with an air of certainty, 'he appears in the back bedroom there' — and that was the bedroom where I'd seen him!

Later on I did tell a Cornish friend, George Ching, of the ghost affair and he knew all about it too. 'That cottage you're in has been haunted for years,' he replied. 'In fact there have been dozens of tenants in your cottage, but no one has stayed. There one day and gone the next! The ghost has been seen at a window.'

He went on to tell me the names of local people who had seen him. This information explained a lot to me, for the minister had called and during his visit asked the same question that a few more had asked, 'Are you going to stay here?' I asked the minister why he was asking that and he gave me a similar answer to that of George Ching.

'Well,' he explained, 'when passing at different times I've seen smoke coming from the chimney and thought I'd give the new tenants a week or two to settle in before visiting, but when I have called, the place has been deserted again!'

So from this I surmised that they too had seen the ghost. I asked George, who as a boy had known Sam Littlejohn, if he'd had a violent death or anything. 'No,' he assured me, 'just normal. I think he died in his sleep. He was a widower and went to London now and again to visit a married daughter.' The only thing odd about him that George could remember was that, at the visiting fairs, he liked riding on the children's roundabouts. So it was just one of those inexplicable mysteries. The Catholic priest didn't seem surprised when I related my midnight escapade to him. He told me it was an 'earth bound' spirit. Some said I shouldn't have attacked, but followed him, and he would have led me to a cache of money — the chances I've missed! Anyway, Sam Littlejohn never called again. I don't suppose he could. I'd split him in half!

More strange happenings

Another strange happening in the cottage occurred one night, when there was heavy breathing just outside the bedroom door — deep breathing as if someone was lying on the landing sound asleep. Quietly getting out of bed, I crept to the door, quietly lifted the latch and whipped the door open.

The breathing immediately stopped and the landing was deserted. When I got back into bed, the heavy breathing started again. I repeated the stratagem, but before opening the door, I listened. The breathing was from the floor, just outside. I whipped the door open again. Immediate silence and not a soul there. I went back to bed and was just getting comfortable, when the breathing started again. 'Right, chum,' I thought, 'if you are sound asleep, you cannot be interested in me and I'm certainly not interested in you.' So I went to sleep with the heavy breathing still going on. Probably the ghost and I ended up snoring in unison, but I never fathomed that one out.

'Wilf, there's a rat sitting on the mat in front of the fire!'

It was a Saturday afternoon and I was in the garden digging up potatoes. Charlie was stretched out near me on an old sack, sunning himself. It was my mother calling from the back door. She had come down from the Midlands to spend a week's holiday and was obviously shaken by the discovery.

'I was reading,' she went on, still trembling, 'and felt something moving across the back of the seat, so moved forward, thinking it was the cat. After a while, I happened to glance at the floor and there was a rat, sitting beside my chair.'

'It's all right,' I reassured her, 'it won't hurt you, but all the same it shouldn't be there. I'll take Charlie in and he'll move it.' Picking him up, I carried him through the back door and looked into the room. Sure enough, there was a rat sitting in front of the fire, but I immediately sensed that something was wrong with it. There were two reasons for my assumption. It was in beautiful condition, for its coat had a lovely gloss but all the same, it was far too fat and lethargic. However, it was in my territory and had to be moved. I put the cat down near it. Now the strange thing about any hunting animal is that anything they normally chase must be moving before they can identify it as a quarry. Charlie calmly walked past the rat, jumped onto the chair my mother had vacated and promptly went to sleep. I realised what was wrong with the rat. It had eaten too much from a sack of wheat that I kept in the passage for the poultry and this had swollen its stomach, making it ill. After safely dispatching it, I tried to explain the 'Trinity' to my mother, but she couldn't understand it. In spite of all my explanations, she still couldn't see why a rat should be sitting on a mat in the living room in front of the fire.

'And another thing,' she said, still in a state of shock, 'I felt something crawl over my bed during the night.'

'If it was a rat,' I explained, 'it still wouldn't hurt you. It would be one of the tenants.'

Next morning, she packed her case and caught an early train to Birmingham. 'I think that cottage is haunted as well' were her parting words.

Sitting reading by the fire one evening, I heard paper tearing. The sound of the tearing was coming from the cupboard of the Dutch dresser. The dresser door was slightly ajar and, as I watched, a cheeky little mouse with beady, bright eyes peeped out, then disappeared again. This in itself was innocent enough, but what about Charlie? If the mouse was on night shift all would be well, because Charlie only came in during the day, but this dovetailing of time was too unlikely for it to be true.

As I sat musing and trying to work out a solution to the problem, the mouse kept coming to the dresser door and having a look at me as if to make sure I was in total agreement with the nest building, then, as if on elastic, it would suddenly disappear and the tearing would be resumed. It was the busiest and friendliest mouse I'd ever seen and any creature, however large or small, coming into my domain immediately inspires in my breast a feeling of guardianship, but no matter how I studied the situation, no feasible answer presented itself.

Within a few days, however, what with the normal pressures of life and also being out most evenings, I forgot all about my new tenant until one dinner time, I came in and much to my chagrin, Charlie had caught my new friend! It was sitting in a begging position and was a most pitiful sight, covered in the cat's wet drooling, and panting for breath. As I stood looking in dismay, Charlie pounced again, throwing it up in the air, then pushing the hapless draggled creature with its paw, trying to get it to move. Only one answer came to my mind, 'Put it out of its misery quickly!' Grasping the small fire shovel, I took a swipe at the mouse. Unfortunately, Charlie pounced at the same time and I nearly bonked him instead of the mouse. This happened a couple of times and I was just waiting for another opportune moment when, much to my amazement, the mouse which had seemed half dead, suddenly made a lightning dash for freedom and escaped under the door that led into the passage. Charlie moved fast too, but the mouse beat him to it. I was pleased with the outcome, because my new tenant would probably take the hint and seek new lodgings and Charlie wouldn't be blamed for doing what comes naturally, so that harmony might reign again.

Now, are animals devoid of memory or oblivious to danger? That same night, I was sitting by the fireside when I thought I saw a movement out of the corner of my eye. I looked at the cupboard door and, sure enough, the mouse was back! A little face appeared, had a look (probably to make sure I was all right), then back she went to get on with the housework. However, under the circumstances, it was testing providence too much to leave it in the cupboard and as it was obviously a field mouse, I got a soft, long handled broom and chased it out of the back door. Being an animal, its mental telepathy assured it that no harm was meant, for it certainly didn't want to leave and kept dodging the brush, trying to get back to the cupboard. I found quite a lot of torn paper; in fact I think it liked the tearing sound, but there were no young ones.

Speaking about mental telepathy in animals, a grey squirrel struck up a friendship. At first, he came to the door for nuts and grasped my hand, with all the claws out while he took a nut, but within a few days he no longer used them. Very soon he had the run of the house, but as he liked to sit on the table and was by no means 'house trained', I decided it had to go. However, getting it out was easier said than done! For I discovered that grey squirrels are remarkably quick, tenacious and also self-willed. They only agree if it suits them. One evening, I opened all the doors and windows and tried to chase it out with a handbrush. It thought the attempted eviction was a new game I had thought up. Round and round the room it went. It was on chairs, dresser, window sills, table, with me hitting with the brush just behind it. I had to laugh, for on the table was an open paper bag with nuts in and twice, as it ran past, it had the audacity to grab a nut and transfer it to its mouth without any hesitation as it ran! Its speed was really remarkable. It was so quick and determined to stay in that eventually I gave up the chase. The episode ended with the squirrel sitting on the mantleshelf eating nuts and me sitting on the chair, wishing I'd never let him in. Eventually, I beat him by cunning, for the next time he was out, I closed the doors and windows and if I found him waiting to come in, I'd chase him with a broom. I never fed him again either. But all through this eviction period, he never showed any fear, knowing, as I mentioned before, by mental telepathy that I meant him no harm.

A month after my mother had returned to Birmingham, I wakened up in the night and heard someone creeping up the stairs. I sat up in bed and listened. Creak. Silence. Creak. Silence. Creak. Each wooden step creaked as it took the weight. It sounded more like Two-ton Tessie coming up, than a phantom. Eventually it got to the top of the landing. I expected the bedroom latch to be lifted and someone to walk in, but nothing happened.

Suddenly I remembered that my brother and his little son had arrived that day to spend a holiday and for the moment, I'd completely forgotten about them. I guessed that he had been down to the loo and was quietly returning to bed. As I lay down again, I thought that I must be getting ghosts on the brain. Next morning I told him about my lapse of memory and wondered who it was creeping up the stairs.

'Well,' he replied, 'I can add to that, by telling you what happened when I got back to the bedroom. It was such a bright, moonlight night, that I went over to the window to admire the scene. It was nearly clear as daylight when I looked out, sheep in the neighbouring fields were giving an occasional tremulous 'Baa' and in the distance I could discern the sea and even the white line of the waves. Looking up the road, I saw what I made out to be as they approached, two dogs trotting along. I watched them get nearer and nearer, then instead of coming on and passing the cottage, they took a long detour along the hedges before joining the road again. They seemed to be avoiding the cottage.'

I told him that I thought I had the answer to his riddle, for I had acquired a dog or rather a bitch called Pat. She was a collie-retriever cross and one night there had been such a howling at the back door that I immediately opened it and in shot Pat with her hair standing on end with fright. She was just past the puppy stage and she sat on my knee for an hour or more before I could induce her to sit on the floor. Something had given her a mighty big fright! She might of course have seen Sammy Littlejohn, but what I surmised to have happened was that these two dogs had come for a spot of courting and Pat, who hadn't a clue about the facts of life, had taken them for canine ghosts, peering at her at the back of the cottage in the moonlight and had gone berserk with fright. I think my guess was correct, for whenever I saw the dogs, they seemed to have a guilt complex and if Pat was with me, she would make sure I was between her and them.

I liked Pat very much but cannot say the same about all carnivores. I once knew a West Indian whose father had bred dogs all his life and he said a dog was always more aggressive towards a nervous person because the latter had more adrenalin in the blood and a dog, being a hunter by nature, senses and scents this, which arouses its 'killer instinct'. All carnivores are killers. These animals, as opposed to the peaceful herbivores, will either have to reform their diet as the karma of the planet progresses or they will be wiped out as alien life. Flesh-eating humans are in a similar dilemma, for while we live and eat by the rule of savagery, so will our progress to better things be retarded.

Some time ago, there was a interesting film of wildlife shown on television. It depicted a lioness stalking and then trying to kill a deer. There was a running commentary by a ranger whose explanation of the sequence of events held me spellbound. A hunting animal, he told us, always goes for one separated from the herd and the stag, the herd leader, knew this and accepted the risk of death, to save the weaker members. In this instance, filmed through a telescopic lens in hilly woodland, the lioness glided stealthily in and out of the cover of trees, following the stag which ran on a lower level. 'Now,' broke in the commentator, 'he will find a niche in the rocks or bank where he is protected from the rear, then turn and face his pursuer.' Indeed, this is exactly what happened. The stag placed himself in a position where high rocks prevented a rear attack, then quite calmly turned to face the lioness. Increasing her speed and running in a crouching, feline motion, she quickly caught up with her quarry and with amazing speed and ferocity, attacked his flank from the side. The stag nimbly countered the attack by lowering his antlers and side stepping. The lioness skidded to a halt to prevent getting impaled, then with equal speed, flashed around to attack from the other side. Again the stag swung round with lowered antlers. The lioness, in a killing fury, attacked again and again, but always came up against the antlers. In the end she became exhausted and the stag, sensing this and realising he now had the upper hand, suddenly turned the tables and chased the lioness, who ran away with her tail between her legs. The last we saw of this fascinating drama was the stag skipping nimbly up the hill to rejoin the herd. The photography and commentary of this natural episode was most interesting, but what struck me most was the lesson it taught of the tactics used by the carnivore compared to those of the herbivore. One had all the fury and hate necessary to kill, the other was merely defensive, yet proved superior.

The predatory animal, bird or fish which lives by plunder and pillage ending in the death of the victim is by nature cowardly, for it only attacks the weaker and always from the rear. Flesh-eating animals usually attack in packs too, relying on the safety of numbers. Even domesticated dogs abandoned by their owners and left in derelict areas revert to this inborn instinct and form packs.

Jacques Cousteau, the underwater naturalist and photographer, says this cowardly trait applies even to vicious sharks. Face an oncoming shark in the water and make an aggressive movement or shout and it will by-pass the attack, but turn and try to swim away — you're a gonner! I wouldn't like to try it myself, but it must be true because I've seen Cousteau on TV lunge at an oncoming shark with his camera. Before disembarking at Freemantle docks in Australia, we watched a shark swimming near the stern of the ship and its speed was fantastic. One flick of the tail and it shot away as if jet propelled, then another flick and it was back again. I certainly wouldn't have fancied my chances in the water with it!

Have humans adopted these bully-coward traits? Much to our woe, I think we have. In war, for instance, the strategy is to avoid a frontal attack and strike at the enemy's flank. We see the predatory pack instinct on the football terraces when gangs of hooligans, inflamed by their 'killer' diet, attack, maim and destroy for the sheer joy of it. We have baby battering and the sad spectacle of special houses for women who have to be protected from their husbands. Always the stronger attacks the weaker: the bully-coward trait of the carnivore.

Anna Kingsford, the illuminated reformer of the Victorian era, had this to say in a lecture on vegetarianism: 'People talk to me sometimes about the peace conventions and ask me to join societies for putting down war. I always say, "You are beginning at the wrong end, putting the cart before the horse. If you want people to leave off fighting like beasts of prey, you must first get them to leave off living like beasts of prey. You cannot reform institutions without first reforming men".'

Voltaire said, 'Men feeding upon carnage and drinking strong drinks, all have an empoisoned and acrid blood which drives them mad in a hundred different ways.' And Thomas Hardy gets down to the fundamentals when he says, 'The establishment of the common origin of all species involves the readjustment of altruistic morals, by enlarging the Golden Rule from the area of mere mankind to that of the whole animal kingdom.'

We are what we eat and if we eat by the gun and knife, we will live in that mentality, but on the non-harming, fruitarian diet, a harmonious state prevails throughout the whole being and a feeling of unity with all life ensues. With a change of diet, the negative forces of envy, greed, jealousy, hate and brutality would slowly change to the positive forces of harmony and goodwill and diseases of the mind as well as of the body would be no more. If you doubt the logic of this, try it for yourself, and see. The unhappy childhood of my own family and of countless others could have been a happy period, heralding a peaceful, harmonious adulthood and for this Utopia to become a reality only needs a switch of diet.

The hens take over

'Watch your hens,' a farmer called out to me one evening as I got off the scooter after gardening in the village. 'There are foxes around.'

Later, when I went up to the store, Mr Elton warned me too. 'Keep your hens in for a while, there's a fox around. I lost six of mine last night.' This news was startling. Because my hens had been reared from chicks, there were nearly a hundred now and they hadn't laid an egg yet. They were living like lords, or rather ladies, and I was living in penury. For a fox to play havoc now would ruin all my chances of affluence. Besides, my hens were not ordinary hens, for each had its own personality. Some were curious, while others couldn't care less, some aggressive, others placid. The back door of the cottage was like a stable door — in two halves — and one hen that I called 'Keyhole Kate' used to sit nearly all day on the closed lower half, looking into the living room, making sure she didn't miss anything.

'Streaker', another of the flock, caused some anxiety. For some obscure reason, she was in a permanent moult from the waist down, or rather, from the waist to the rear, and her favourite pastime was to be chased by motor cars. Why this particular hen chose this particular form of recreation, mystified me, but I always felt slightly embarrassed when she streaked past the window. During the summer, a lot of American tourists used to visit Cornwall and I frequently heard 'toot-tooting' and, looking out of the window, I would see Streaker, head down, with featherless 'parson's nose' stuck up in the rear, having a whale of a time zig-zagging down the road with a flash American car crawling along behind. She raced until she reached the end of the garden, then ran through the hedge. Ten minutes later, I would hear the screech of brakes again and there was Streaker zig-zagging the other way in assumed terror. If there is such a word as modesty, Streaker didn't know about it and what is more, she didn't want to know. It says a lot for the drivers that she was not run over.

If foxes were around, immediate action was called for. The coop in use was falling apart and as the cost of a new one was out of the question, only

one solution to the problem presented itself. The hens must share the cottage with me. Next day, I chopped down saplings from a nearby copse and hung them from the beams in the stone flagged sitting room. I covered the settee and easy chairs with old curtains and sacking and before darkness fell, the new tenants moved in. They loved it! There were cabbages and sprouts hanging by string from the beams, two galvanised tubs with food, hay spread on the floor and, around the inglenook, six orange boxes with straw inside for them to lay their eggs in. Some of my tenants sat on the settee, others preferred the easy chairs, but the more conventional used the swinging perches. I also gave them my one and only oil stove to keep warm, because the February gales were still howling around the cottage. So, from then on, while they lived in perfect bliss, I sat with my overcoat on in the fireless living room, waiting for the first egg.

They were all about nine months old now and due to start laying at any time. In the evenings, I lit the calor gas stove in their room, hoping they would think it was the rising sun and so speed up their reproductive desires. Time and time again, there were false alarms. While reading or writing, I was conscious of the ruffling of feathers and poultry noises coming from the next room, when suddenly there would be a loud and repeated fast clucking, ending in a long drawn out *cluuurrrk* and a vigorous flapping of wings. I jumped off the chair, inwardly shouting, 'Hallelujah. Praise the Lord. It's an egg!' and make a dash for the sitting room. As soon as they heard me coming, all the noise stopped abruptly and when I entered the room, heads all turned sideways with one eye watching. Silent. Motionless. Carefully stepping over to the inglenook, I got on my hands and knees and crawled around the orange boxes, feeling inside each one for an egg, and drew a blank. Still silent, they watched me go out again, absolutely fascinated by my antics. They couldn't make it out. To them, I was just going through some strange religious ritual or I was just plain 'loco'. No sooner had I got back into my chair, when the egg-laying call sounded again. 'Cluck, cluck, cluck, cluck — *cluuurrrk*' followed by a vigorous flapping of wings. I leapt up again, thanked everyone in heaven, dashed into their room and as usual, drew a blank.

Now my hens were by no means daft and soon cottoned on to the fact that whenever this particular sound was made it brought me into their midst. So no sooner was this discovery made, than they acted upon it and as they undoubtedly liked my company (probably taking me for an eccentric uncle or something) made my life a succession of frustrating hopes and disappointments. Especially in the evenings, the usual poultry noises in the next room left me unperturbed, until one gave an egg-laying call. Everything became silent. All ears, I knew, were listening to hear if I was coming. Should I go? Should I not? Was it an egg this time or were they having their usual game? If I didn't go in, they slowly resumed their fluttering and preening. Then that tantalising call came again. Immediate silence! All the commotion stopped while they listened. When I went in on a fruitless errand, the silence continued until they heard me settle in the kitchen again, then pandemonium broke out. There was cackling and squawking and I could hear some violently flapping their wings as they nearly fell off their perches with glee. I'd been caught again!

And so it went on, night after night. I should mention that my hens never seemed to mind being crowded into the sitting room. When I was in, usually at week ends, I opened the door and window so that they could go out if they wished, but they didn't seem keen to leave the room. One or two might go through the open window to peck around nearby in the garden, and the few that came out of the door remained with me in the living room. They seemed more scared of missing anything than wanting freedom. When the few outside heard me go into their room, they couldn't get back quickly enough and they obviously weren't bothered when the door and window were closed again. Of course, it is not all hens that have a settee and easy chairs to sit on, an oil stove to warm their feet and the gas lit every night in case they are nervous. Except for Streaker, they were all fat, glossy feathered and care free, while I sat in the next room, living on tins of baked beans and boiled winter kale in an attempt to keep body and soul together.

My only square meal was on a Sunday when I had finished going around the villages on my scooter delivering the Sunday papers, for on that day Molly, a widow living with her little daughter, invited me to dinner and to spend the rest of the day at her place. She worked at the Manor House and in return, as part payment, she lived rent free in a converted loft. Even with this meal, I was in such a state of emaciation that if galloping consumption had struck, I wouldn't have lasted a week, for with the countryside still in the grip of winter, gardening jobs were intermittent and nearly every penny coming in was going out in food for the poultry. Also I was a month overdue on the rent and to add to my woe the calor gas cylinder was running out. Hence my desperation for the hens to start laying. I even started dreaming about eggs. Sometimes they were lovely dreams. Dreams that I was filling baskets with eggs. At other times I had nightmares, that I had sat on the flippin' things. However, all good things come to he who waits.

One evening, it was dark when I returned from work, so I went straight into the sitting room and lit the calor gas and lo! — on the settee was an egg! It was the biggest egg I have ever seen. I picked it up to make sure it was real. Sure enough it was an egg. A real egg! I was over the moon with the dual emotions of joy and relief. My financial worries were over. This was the start of untold wealth. The hens were all dead silent, motionless, looking alternately at the egg, then at me. I looked at each hen in turn, trying to get some clue as to which one had laid it, so that I could give it a great big sloppy kiss, but my hens were all born poker players. All I got from the eye of each one in turn was a look of non-committal denial. 'It wasn't me!' 'It wasn't me!' I don't think they were quite sure whether laying an egg was the proper thing to do.

I couldn't eat it. It was too precious. I thought, 'I'll give it to Molly!' and jumping on my scooter, went post-haste to the Manor House with my precious gift wrapped safely in a cloth.

'Molly,' I called, pushing open the door, 'I've brought you an egg. It's from one of my hens!'

'Oh, thanks, Wilf,' she called back, coming down the stairs, still brushing her hair, 'Will you stay for supper?'

'I've brought you an egg,' I repeated, holding it out as if it was the Koh-I-Noor. It's the first egg!'

'Oh, thanks a lot.' she took the proffered offering but hardly gave it a second glance, 'I'll have it for breakfast. Now you are here you might as well stay for supper.'

I felt a bit crestfallen. 'Thanks, Molly, yes I'd like to.' I had expected her to go berserk with excitement. Really, being a woman, she didn't realise the enormity of the event. Now that one of my hens had laid an egg, life as we knew it on this planet would never be the same again. She was more interested in the supper, than the egg. But on the other hand, I suppose it was expecting too much for a woman to go into raptures because a starry-eyed suitor had presented her with an egg.

It was nearly midnight when I got back to the cottage. All the hens were silent, listening to my return. I rushed straight in to see if there were any more eggs, and behold, there were three more! One on an easy chair and two more in corners of the room. My look of beatific joy must have conveyed to them the realisation that egg-laying was something of which to be proud, for they started milling around me and their clucking held a distinct note of promise. All of a sudden the room seemed to take on a rosier hue.

From now on, the eggs came thick and fast. 'Right,' they seemed to say, 'If it's eggs you want, it's eggs you'll have!' There were eggs everywhere; on the settee, the armchairs, the inglenook, the floor. I was picking up eggs like cherries. The only place they didn't lay was in the specially provided orange boxes. There were eggs on top, in front, but never inside for they had associated them with their uncle's queer ritual and were therefore taboo for laying in.

Two days after the avalanche started, I stopped the Egg Marketing Board van as it passed the door and asked the driver if he would include me in his round.

'When are you in for me to pick them up?' he asked, 'Saturday morning all right?'

'Yes — ideal for me.'

'Right, take a few boxes and egg trays to be getting on with,' and coming to the back of the van, took out three boxes and some trays. 'See you Saturday morning,' he called as he got back into the driver's seat, 'and don't forget to clean the eggs.' I watched the receding van until it disappeared around a bend in the road. I was in big business now!

Now in this vale of tears there is usually, I have found, a negative aspect that seems to loom up in opposition to unbridled joy, a sort of counter force that casts a shadow over any attainment — and, in my case, the shadow came in the form of a rapid drop in egg prices. The flood of eggs from my hens evidently triggered off something that sent all the other hens in Great Britain laying in abundance too. After the first batch of eggs had gone to the grading station, I read in the Sunday papers that the price had dropped sharply and, within a fortnight, the price was just over a quarter of what it had been.

Reluctantly, I realised that my venture into poultry keeping had fizzled out, my own little South Sea Bubble had burst, for at this price, after paying for food, paraffin and calor gas, my profit would be nil. The choice was either to keep my feathered friends and to continue to live on baked beans, or to cut my losses by selling the birds and resuming a normal diet. Very reluctantly, I decided upon the latter course. Besides, they couldn't live permanently in the sitting room.

At this time, a rather pleasant incident occurred that made me realise the intimacy that must prevail in a small community. I seem always to be concerned and centred on my own affairs, so that anything or anyone outside my own sphere just does not exist. Nevertheless, much more is known about one another's business and ways of life than a self-centred person like myself even imagines. As I said, my own troubles and trials left me little time to interest myself in other people's affairs, yet others in the neighbourhood must have known about my trials and tribulations with the hens than I gave them credit for.

On the fourth Saturday morning of delivering eggs to the Marketing Board, the van driver called as usual to pick up the boxes.

'Call any time during the week,' he told me as he loaded up, 'Payment is monthly and your cheque should be ready'

'Right,' I answered, trying to sound cheerful, for my anticipation of monetary gain was, as I said before, somewhat dampened by my frequent assessment of profit and loss as the price had dropped, 'I'll call in on Friday.'

It had just turned five o'clock when I got off the scooter. The van driver was talking to the manager at the entrance to the factory. When I walked over, he introduced me to the latter: an easy-going good natured type and, after chatting for a while, he asked me into the office to collect the cheque. As we walked through the door, about twenty women and girls working at benches, gave a spontaneous cheer when they recognised me. I was somewhat startled and looked at the manager. 'That cheer for you?'

He smiled as he looked at me. 'No. For you!'

This little episode pleasantly surprised me, for it conveyed a feeling of local goodwill that I was at last drawing money in return for my efforts, but this was countered by the rather uncomfortable feeling that they knew all about my hens sitting on the settee in my best room!

'Mr Goodburn from Marhamchurch will call in the morning and pick up the poultry, Mr Crone.' I had gone to the general store and Mr Elton, always a good friend, had arranged for a farmer to buy the lot and although the price offered was quite fair, it was now a case of trying to recoup some of my losses. Early the next morning, a Land Rover pulling a large covered trailer drew up at the cottage door. A bulky red faced farmer got out.

'Got some hens for me, I believe.'

'Yes, that's right. They're in the sitting room.'

He must have been a bit deaf.

'Where?'

'In the sitting room.'

'Can I see them?'

'Certainly. Come in.' Now time and again I had warned my young hens not to have anything to do with strange men. My admonition now backfired, for as soon as the farmer entered the room, they all went berserk with fright. It was bedlam; flapping wings, squawking birds zigzagging through the air and dashing themselves against walls and furniture in a frenzy of fear. As soon as the farmer hastily quitted the room, peace was immediately restored, but they were all distressed and motionless, looking at me with an obvious question in their eyes, 'Who was that?'

'Bring one or two out and I'll have a look at them,' he called from outside the door. I took out two; one in each arm. He was pleased with their appearance. 'Yes, they're all right. I'll bring in one crate at a time to hold ten. Fill it near the door and we'll carry them out to the trailer.' And so went my hens. My heart sank as the truck revved up to take them away. Back in the living room, I sat looking at the cheque the farmer had given me. It didn't mean anything. In fact, I felt as if I'd forsaken friends for cash. Already the cottage sounded quiet and empty. I remembered the fun Streaker had, zig-zagging up and down the road, the false egg-laying calls and the hens' fascination as I crawled on all fours looking for non-existent eggs. I could only hope they would be happy in their new home.

Charlie goes missing

I sat musing a while. A rat scuttled along the skirting boards. This reminded me that Charlie had been missing for over a week, a most unusual length of time for him. Being a tom, he was in the habit of staying away for two or three days and then spending a couple of days with me, but he was never away for more than three days. I was worried. Farmers set traps in the hedges for rabbits, foxes, rats or anything else that could be caught. Perhaps he had been trapped. After work, in the evenings, I went around the neighbouring fields calling his name, but got no answering 'miaow'. Charlie had a very quiet voice, so I stood at intervals listening after I had called, but I got no reply. All was silent.

About this time, there was an amusing incident which was certainly funny for me, but not for the other party. The front door of the cottage was nearly square. It could be termed 'chunky' as it was short, wide and of very thick wood and, with the heavy, insecure stonework above the lintel, it frequently jammed. Within a day or two of shaving wood off the top or bottom, it would jam again. I stopped taking off more wood for it became obvious that the door itself was acting as a prop to hold up the building. If too much was taken off, the whole crazy cottage might collapse. To counter this possible calamity, I attached a stout rope to the inner handle and when a visitor called, I heaved on the rope to open it, then shut it as quickly as possible before the stone lintel could drop.

It was late one Sunday afternoon in the autumn and I had arrived back from delivering the papers. The sky was dull and heavy with snow clouds. An eerie, drifting mist swirled around the cottage. Before going to Molly's,

I sat in the twilight reading one of the papers which hadn't been sold. Subconsciously, while reading, I thought I heard a gentle tapping at intervals. I went to the door to see if anyone was there. As I looked out, two eyes appeared at the other side. 'Ah, so there is someone there!' Grasping the rope, I heaved the door open and on the threshold stood a hatless boy scout with his hair literally standing on end with fright. 'Cu — cu — could I have my bi-billy can filled with water, please?' he stammered.

'Certainly, sonny,' I replied in a casual voice, trying to allay his fear and let him see I wasn't a ghost. I filled it at the pump in the kitchen and took it back to him. 'Is that full enough?'

'Yes, th-thanks.' He took the can and walked away, but for two pins he would have taken to his heels and run like mad from the haunted cottage. I guessed what had happened. He had knocked two or three times and, getting no answer, thought the lonely, derelict looking building must be empty. Then out of curiosity he had looked through the door and had seen two spooky eyes peering at him from the inside. No wonder he was shaken! But he was brave for, scared as he was, he stood his ground and did his best to look unaffected.

Healing power

Charlie had been missing for three weeks now. I still went around the hedges, but hope of finding him was fading. However, it was past eleven o'clock one night, when I thought there was a faint 'miaow' from outside the back door. It was so faint that I thought it might be my imagination, but I went out to make sure — and there was my poor cat, with one paw raised, just a bedraggled skeleton of his former self. He was plastered with mud and dried sweat.

Gently I picked him up and carried him in. Obviously he had been caught in a trap, for one of his front paws had been literally torn from the leg. He must have pulled and pulled for days and nights until he had freed himself by severing the paw from the leg. I heated some water and put in a little disinfectant, then gently bathed the shreds of skin and congealed blood. It must have been extremely painful, to say the least, but he never flinched. Cats are true stoics. After cleaning the wound, I carefully bandaged it and hoped for the best, but Charlie reacted to my bandaging in a similar manner as had the chicken. As soon as I sat him on a comfortable cushion, he immediately started to lick and lick at the bandage. By next morning he had removed it and was licking the raw stump. Again I bathed and bandaged it, a little more firmly this time, but within a few hours he had it off again and was licking the raw flesh. This ritual was repeated so often that in the end I realised he did not wish it to be covered, so I decided to leave Charlie and nature to effect a cure.

Evidently animals prefer their own built-in doctoring rather than external assistance. Day after day he licked and licked at the raw shank with its slivers of raw flesh, until I wondered if I had been right to give up the bandaging, because a cat's tongue is very rough and it might keep the wound open. However, within a week he had got rid of the shreds of flesh and the wound looked healthier. In a fortnight, it seemed to be conforming more to shape, and so it continued without respite in the licking and believe me, after about three months, a complete new paw had grown! The only parts missing were the claws. He never grew them again, but apart from that he was completely mobile.

Mentioning the cat healing its paw reminds me of an incident concerning an expedition to the South Polar seas many years ago. It happened in the Falklands Islands, where the natives were allowed on ship, but soon became a nuisance by stealing. In the end, the crew had to fire at them with muskets to warn them off and during such a skirmish, a baby in its mother's arms was hit by a bullet. The ship's company, feeling remorseful, had them taken aboard where the doctor cleaned and bandaged the baby's arm. Unfortunately, after repeated treatments, the wound turned septic and inflammation spread around the area. Later, the doctor stopped treating the child because the mother started to take the bandages off and continually to lick the wound. Within a fortnight, during which time the ship was tied up to the wharf for loading and unloading, the doctor found that the child's wound had completely healed — such is the healing power of saliva! Have you noticed too, that if you cut a finger, you put it straight into your mouth!

There is no doubt that the most effective healer is within ourselves and if we eat fermenting fruit and vegetation instead of putrefactive meat and dairy produce, then we can resist any infection. Before I became a fruitarian, any thorn entering the flesh became surrounded by pus. It now becomes surrounded by clear fluid. Mucous from the nasal cavity used to be discoloured with pus. Now it is clear. So these are clear indications that my body is cleared of putrefactive suppuration. My father and brother and sister died of cancer years ago, yet there is no sign of disease in my body and I'm not bragging, mind, just stating facts. Of course life on a reformed diet is not a bed of roses. We still have the trials and tribulations of the world to contend with, but at least we haven't a sick body to add to our woes.

In all my dealings with animals, I have found little difference from humans in their reactions to love, fear or pain. Their only failing, as far as I can see, is their lack of sympathy if one is sick or injured. The leader of any group will protect the herd, and the herd will team up against a common enemy; also the females will protect their young, but I have seen an animal dying, yet others casually pass by, obviously lacking in sympathy. Herds usually seek food in a ranging circle. This applies not only to wild life, but to such animals as cows or sheep in a restricted area.

When one is nearing its life-span, it will lie down while the rest pass on and perhaps join them again next time round, but its excursions with the rest of the herd become less frequent until, in the end, it lies prostrate and sinks into a final sleep. Herbivores are in no pain or distress during this final period for I have, at odd times, rubbed them on the forehead and they wake up dreamily and start chewing the cud quite placidly again. They are merely fulfilling a cycle of life and nature which, to any original Edenic creature, is never cruel. The animal living on fermentative vegetation has no pathogenic virus within it to start a painful, putrefactive disease or fever as the body weakens. On the other hand, a predatory animal, living by killing others, often dies being eaten by an internal putrefactive virus. Our own bodies, being no whit different from that of the creatures, come under the same inexorable law of cause and effect so that from a health and ethical point of view, the man or woman living on Edenic food scores all round.

It has been pointed out that many saintly people have been predatory in their mode of life so, some say, there cannot be much wrong with the diet from the celestial aspect, yet there must be an imbalance. Let us look at this paradox from the accepted theory of wave frequencies. If we agree that the material wave is denser than the spiritual, then the saint who nourishes his body on dead flesh and animal by-products, must be operating under the strain of two opposing waves. His spirit is in sympathy with the rarefied radiations emanating from the higher planes, while his earthly vehicle is tuned to the dense radiations emanating from brutality and death. It is, to say the least, an imbalance, a contradiction that would take a very clever deity to explain away. Invariably you will find that what is ethically or spiritually correct is also correct on the outer material planes.

Since man left Eden, we now have the paradox of living as predators and thereby creating diseases in ourselves, then crucifying animals in countless thousands, trying to find a cure for the inevitable diseases caused by eating them. An evil circle that only a return to the Edenic, fruit eating diet can break. Unfortunately the two main stumbling blocks to the solution of this predicament are the clergy and the medicos, for neither has a balanced view. The former searching the ether, looking for a nebulous entity that will cure all diseases of the mind and body, and the latter peering through a microscope for the cause in a virus.

Visitors

Gypsies and tramps used to call at the cottage occasionally. Tramps seemed to work a regular circuit, for the same ones appeared at regular intervals. After I had been at the cottage a few months, I noticed a small piece of red ribbon attached to a twig in the hedge about a hundred yards each side of the cottage. This, I suspected was a sign to the fraternity that a call was worthwhile, for, having tasted some of the life myself while in Australia, I seldom let them go away empty handed. One tramp asked if he could sleep on the floor. It was late on a cold winter evening when he called, so I let him sleep on the thick rug mat in front of the fire. Next morning, when I came down the stairs, it was hard to tell which was the rag mat and which was the tramp. I gave him breakfast, but conversation was out of the question, for the only response I got to my perfunctory remarks were grunts and wheezes issuing from a bronchial chest. However, I did notice that these 'gentlemen of the road' were never greedy, for they accepted what was offered, then went on their way.

One Saturday afternoon, I was in the garden planting potatoes, when a movement caused me to look up. Two eyes peered at me from a head covered with an abundance of shaggy, ginger hair. It was a bit disconcerting, but the same tramp had called two or three times during the past couple of years and as his eyes were broadset and honest, I wasn't particularly worried. As on previous occasions, he held out a tin can with tea and sugar and politely asked if he could have it filled with hot water. While the water was heating up on the calor gas, I wrapped up half a loaf, some butter and four eggs to help him on his way. When the water had boiled, I filled his can and handed it to him together with the parcel of food. He took the can carefully by the wire handle, thanked me politely, then started to move away. 'Some food for the road,' I said, holding the parcel further out.

He looked around quite placidly. 'No, thank you,' he smiled gently, 'I'm not begging, you know.'

He called about twice a year and was always the same; polite but firm in accepting only the hot water.

Many of these nomadic people struck me as being 'naturals'. They had found the rat race a mode of life so contrary to their nature that they had abandoned it for the open road and a life free from the restrictions of set times and the cares of worldly possessions. They were usually gentle and they phlegmatically accepted the fact that the world classed them as 'wasters'. Come to think of it, their philosophy was also mine, for I had worked in a factory and always considered the stress, noise, and working to the clock as being totally alien to what life should be. Perhaps that, together with my Australian experiences, were the reasons for my sympathy towards them. Of course, sometimes, one knocked at the door and his whole attitude warned me that a scrounger stood on the threshold. 'Got a couple of bob, guv'nor, to help me along?' he would brashly ask, but this type got short shrift and went on his way as poor as he came.

A woman tramp used to intrigue me. Normally, she came by at around six in the evening when I was having tea. She passed the window carrying two sacks, one under each arm, then walked by the window again in the opposite direction, empty handed. Next, she passed the window yet again, staggering along with two more nondescript sacks bulging with 'God-knows-what'. One summer evening when I saw her, out of curiosity, I went upstairs to look out of the bedroom window to watch her progress along the dusty road. What she did was to carry two sacks past two already in the hedge, lay the two she was carrying about a hundred yards further on, then return for the two she had passed, and so on. Her progress to the next village must have been a feat of endurance for it was five miles away and how far she had already humped the sacks, goodness knows! I asked Mr Elton at the store if he had any idea as to where she was going and he was pretty sure that she sold second hand clothes at the villages on market days. She never called for anything and I never asked her if she would like a cup of tea, because I soon found that tramps are wary of proffered help or kindness. They live in a world of their own and if they don't approach you, it is best to leave them alone.

During our travels, Joe and I once stayed with 'down-and-outs', who were the nearest approach to tramps one could get in Australia. We found they were amazingly considerate to one another and nothing was stolen from amongst themselves. Tobacco and food were given to the less fortunate and there was always a good fire burning in an old incinerator throughout the night. We rubbed shoulders with real characters during our stay, yet the atmosphere was always one of goodwill. We stayed in a derelict barn and two old men, quite evidently friends, were an unending source of interest and amusement, for one never answered the other's questions, or even mumbled a thanks for anything. More surprising was the fact that his friend never seemed to expect an answer — so wasn't disappointed! In the light of early dawn, one would sit up, fumble in the pocket of a tattered overcoat which served as a blanket, to withdraw a tin of tobacco and papers and after methodically rolling two cigarettes, lit one for himself and laid the other by the side of his mate's straw pallet. After a while, the other sat up, looked with bleary eyes at the rest of the fraternity in the barn, giving intermittent bronchial coughs as he did so, then sit deliberating the new day.

'Bad night?' enquired the one smoking, with some concern in his voice, but the other took not the slightest notice. Silence reigned for a good time, then: 'Yer coughed a lot in the night.' No answer. Silence, then 'Have a fag — a rolled yer a fag.' Still no answer. Slowly the silent one roused himself enough to pick up the cigarette by his side. The other threw matches over. 'Yer coughed badly last night' No answer, and so it went on. In the end, I got worried in case the silent one did answer. I'm sure the other one would have dropped down dead from fright!

One youth in the barn had a mania for keeping a good pair of trousers well creased. He wore raggy dungarees, a very torn red shirt and a yellow straw hat and every night and morning he went through the same ritual. Religiously, every night, he folded these grey flannels with meticulous care, put them under the blanket he slept on, then, in the morning, lovingly and lingeringly looked at them and stroked the creases down the front with a look of beatific satisfaction. They were either his last link with respectability or ready to conquer a girl should he start courting. He wanted me to accompany him one night after darkness had set in to steal and kill a goat, but I strongly advised him against it. Night was an experience never to be forgotten, for when everyone had sorted and taken the lumps out of their straw, thrown tattered coats and blankets over themselves and settled down to sleep, the nocturnal lullaby began. What with all the wheezing, gurgling, snoring and farting going on, it sounded like a majestic organ playing throughout the night.

There was one other experience in the cottage that I should mention. It was ghostly but quite pleasant. I had wakened just as the day was dawning and was surprised to see another bed in the room, to the left and a little higher than mine. It was a double bed with a young man in a dark green jerkin, whom I instinctively knew to be a doctor, sitting at the foot. Obviously he was very happy and spoke with animation to someone in the bed, but from my lower position, I couldn't see the person he was speaking to. I sat up to get a better view and beheld a woman of about thirty years of age, with long black hair. From her pallid colour, she appeared to be recuperating after some illness, for she lay passive and smiled wanly at her admirer's animated talk. As I looked, the scene gradually faded away, but if I ever saw two people in love — they were!

I have read that ghosts are emanations or phantoms having no real existence. Every event that has taken place on earth has an astral counterpart or picture in the magnetic light and the appearance of ghosts, scenes and whatnot are but the shadows of former times left on the protoplasmic mirror. Even the aborigines of Australia are very conscious of ghosts. It is evidently an interest, tinged with fear, that is common to all humanity. Every night, as darkness set in, fires would be lit around the aboriginal camps to keep the ghosts of the departed away. When an old or sick member of the tribe was obviously soon to depart this world, they removed the body a long way from the camp and left the hot sun to accomplish the 'coup-de-grace', for they believed that the spirit of the departed would return to the camp — if it could be found!

And now, dear reader, having unfolded my experiences with both humans and animals, I would like you to bear with me while I summarise the logic and belief that now guides my life which, I would like to add, has been acquired by using common sense and observation, unfettered by dogma.

UNIVERSAL HARMONY

U NIVERSAL HARMONY OPERATES for Muslim, Jew, Gentile or Communist and the fact that an adherent has a creed can be a stumbling block to that harmony.

I don't believe in an external God, as the churches so rigorously try to uphold by calling on us to have 'blind faith' (with emphasis on both words). What I do believe in is a universal harmony, and to protect myself I have to adhere to its rules, or suffer in consequence. However, beware! Don't fall into the trap of saying, 'Well, universal harmony is God,' because immediately you localise an existing fact into a non-existent unity. If a child gets too near the edge of a cliff, the law of gravity comes into operation and the child is either hurt or killed. If a person wishes to commit suicide and jumps off the edge of a cliff, the same law of gravity applies. So natural laws operate regardless of the individual or the intent. These laws of nature are dominant, uncompromising and must be obeyed. Go without food: we die. Go without water or air: we also die, and so on. If we transgress these laws, we suffer, whether we do it in ignorance or with intent. Abuse any of these fundamental laws, then it has a detrimental rebound according to the severity of the abuse and, although the effects may not be immediately apparent, they eventually build up into some form of retribution. We are part of nature and not an elevated species above its laws. Universal harmony is absolute, perfect and applies to everything created. It bows to neither creed nor dogma in its operation. Religions cause conflict: universal harmony brings peace.

I certainly believe there are forces of good and evil in the ethereal world helping or assailing us, as the case may be, during our earthly existence. Positive, good forces are helping to keep our aim in life steadfast, but are countered by negative, evil spirits which not only try but do rock the boat at times with remarkable and terrifying success. The nearest simile to these spirits is that of a giggling person. Evil entities that giggle in diabolic glee when they cause friction and discord or in any way delay the return to original harmony and the Edenic way of life: spirits of mischief who are ever active. Place a mole on the surface and it will immediately dig its way down, away from the light. In the same way there are forces living in darkness that don't want man to advance; forces that want killing, disease, insanity and turmoil to continue. Negative entities that will do all in their power to prevent enlightenment, that will prevent logical thought, that will oppose to the last such an Edenic diet as fruitarianism because of the far reaching benefits it will bring. It is hard to believe that such entities exist, but they do, for, like the mole, they are denizens of darkness.

Man, being the only medium for harmony in the material manifestation, must use his intellect to improve conditions wherever possible and not rely on some nebulous, exterior force to do it for him, for in this sense, man is God. Unfortunately, the Church will have none of this. It says that only through prayer, adherence to the Bible and dogmas can man hope to advance, yet this very rigidity is proving its own fallibility for even those passages in the Bible which don't conform to the Church's teaching are ignored. Ask any minister why the Church doesn't advocate a fruitarian diet, when it is specifically told to be man's food in Genesis 1:29, and by his various excuses, you'll understand what I mean.

Then, to quote from John 14:26, 'But the Comforter, which is the Holy Ghost, whom the Father will send in my name, he shall teach you all things...' but the Church shuts its ears to any further teachings, and therein lies its weakness. If it were more humble and willing to learn from irrefutable advanced knowledge instead of adopting a 'we know it all' attitude, then the Church would move from strength to strength, but to continue in its present state is to court failure.

No one can deny that the Bible contains a lot of wisdom and sound advice, but to use it as a 'dead end' and to hold countless adherents in archaic bondage, is wrong. It is the case now that public opinion on these matters is more enlightened than the Church!

All religions agree on the fact that everything in the original creation was perfect. That the Garden of Eden was a true state and that the restoration of that state will come about once more. This knowledge apparently derives from a Universal and mutual source of information passed down through the Ages, for not only is it a tenet of Christianity, but also of the Kabala and Oriental religions. Now with harmony, which must embody perfection, there can be no discord: good is harmony; evil is discord. Even in the physical sense, when we do such simple things as cough, it is the natural harmony of the body trying to throw off some unwanted germ or element causing discord. We can carry on up the scale to all the ills to which flesh is heir: fevers, diseases, are all different forms of discord encroaching on original perfection. In the higher, mental sphere, discord is made manifest in the various states of insanity such as killing, abusing, vandalism, sub-normality, addiction, etc.

Now if the logical conception of Origin is that of harmony (and this certainly appears to be the case, for everything in the Universe revolves in a harmonious circle), then in this state of Utopia, discord can have no place. Yet, in recent years, a most mischievous teaching from the East has been gaining credence and that is, that discord is a necessary part of creation; that we cannot have a positive without a negative; joy without sorrow, heat without cold, day without night — and so on. By presenting this line of obvious contrasts, they get a lot of chelas and Western initiates to accept the error that where there is harmony, there must be an opposing force of discord to highlight the harmony! That we must accept disease and war or we couldn't have health and peace, and so on. This is a most mischievous and negative teaching to spring on the unwary. By using the psychology of the salesman and conditioning the mind by a succession of palpable affirmatives, they then slip in a concept which is totally at variance with truth. This is a prime example of how the negative forces use religion to stem enlightenment.

This error was not in the original tenets of the Eastern religions. The Western churches teach no such doctrine, for the Scriptures prophesy the downfall of Satan. So, where the religions of the East have deviated in the acceptance of evil as a necessity, the Western religions have deviated in sacerdotalism and relying on historical records. The original teaching of both East and West was of faultless knowledge, flowing and definite; flowing from the inner to the outer, and not the other way about. Man is capable, through reason and science to apprehend that Eden was an actual primal state of perfection and not a locality. This verity can be reasoned in a very simple way. When we see a rose or any object of beauty, it reacts upon the senses in a most pleasant way; yet dirt and disease or any discord gives a feeling of repugnance and distaste. From where did this criterion, established in our senses, have its origin? Why do we prefer beauty to ugliness, concord to discord, love to hate? It is because we still remember a period in the primordial history of the soul, when beauty and harmony reigned — we remember Eden.

Man has eventually come to the conclusion that the Biblical explanation of the creation of the world fits in with modern knowledge. This, and a Garden of Eden, is among the original tenets of all religions. The peace and tranquility of man's early days in creation are revealed in chapters 1 and

2 of Genesis; 'And the Lord took man and put him into the Garden of Eden to dress it and to keep it.' 'And God said, Behold, I have given you every herb bearing seed, which is upon the face of all the earth, and every tree, in which is the fruit of a tree yielding seed; to you it shall be for food.' This was the beauty of creation that is still latent but not lost in our memory.

This early part of the Bible is now accepted by many. Later on, we obviously get deviation where some of the Hebrew historical events recorded take a large 'pinch of salt' to swallow. However, the fact remains that man was intended to sustain his body from the produce of a garden: from fruit and vegetation and since deviating from this instruction he has brought woe, disease and mental suffering upon himself, for that which is ethically right applies also to the physical. That which applies to the macrocosm applies equally to the microcosm and that which is undeniably correct brings not only bodily health, but mental health too. This instruction on the diet for mankind, given so explicitly in Genesis is now being confirmed by nutritionists, just as the account of creation has now been confirmed by astronomers and scientists.

Food from the garden supplies the body with all the essential nutrients it requires, yet it remains separate from the internal organic structure. This food cannot cause disease to start in the cells. On the other hand, food that comes from the slaughter house or dairy is already being attacked by putrefactive bacteria and, being of a similar structure to the human internal organs can, through putrefaction, create sickness and disease. Remember, a major part of the body's work is in expelling dead cells and putrefactive waste: the very type of food that the unenlightened are continually putting inside their bodies. No wonder the Health Service is cracking under the strain.

Have you realised that all sentient life was originally herbivorous? Yet this was so, for referring again to Genesis 1:30, we read: 'And to every beast of the earth, and to every fowl of the air, and to every thing that creepeth upon the earth, wherein there is life, I have given every green herb for food: and it was so.' No reference here to nature being 'red in tooth and claw', so often quoted by the flesh-eater as if it was a divine declaration of consent for debauchery. Two thirds of the animals that inhabit the earth are still herbivorous, it is only the remaining third that, like man, has fallen in state. This was the original pattern of life in conformity with universal harmony. The Biblical explanation of a God saying this and that, is obviously a convenient synopsis of existing conditions used by some early recorder.

Once, I visited an aquarium with a friend and some of the crab-like creatures caught from the depths of the ocean were positive nightmares even to look at. One in particular had two huge claws with the end of one dividing into a cruel looking curved pincer, the other formed a hammer head. This we were told, was to hammer the luckless victim, held by the pincer claw, to death! If this diabolical monster of the deep was an original and intended creation of a 'God of love', then both the Bible and the dictionary are completely wrong in their definition of the word 'love'. I believe that, far from being created by a God of love, they are the creation, through materialisation, of wrong thought. Just as the drunken man, through an aberration of the brain, is convinced he sees 'pink elephants' so, through generations of killing and abuse of life, have these monstrosities evolved from phantom devils into actual creatures.

Not only is far too much reliance placed upon an ethereal, phantom, external God, but also too blind an acceptance of everything written in the Bible. Too strict an adherence can be a stumbling block to progress. A lot in the Scriptures is undeniably right and logical. This we must heed; but that which is equally illogical must be seen as such and not blindly believed. Much in Leviticus, for instance, is just too stupid for words. Some of the childish ritual and superstition related is worthy of the outpourings of a retarded five-year old. Common sense, on the other hand, when used to good cause, far outstrips both religious and Biblical teachings in action. I will give you an instance

On television, there was a programme showing villages of backward people living in India. Goats and dogs roamed and fouled the area. Sanitation in the hovels and dusty roads was virtually nil and their drinking water came from a stream polluted with excrement. Roughly half the number of babies died during their first year through various infections and illnesses. These deaths were looked upon by the simple, superstitious people as being unavoidable and were blamed on all sorts of external powers: the will of Allah, the wrath of the idols, and so on. After a study of Western methods of hygiene, the Indian government sent health emissaries into the areas and, as a result of their findings, arranged for one person from each village to take a six month course of hygiene and sanitation and then return to the village as a resident health adviser. A woman of about twenty-five years of age, from one of the villages, went on the course.On her return, the attitude of the local people was of apathy mixed with suspicion. Her first job, with the aid of a government grant was to get some of the men to pipe water to the village from a clean source. She taught them to boil all water which came from the stream and instructed other women that breast-feeding was safest. If a bottle had to be used to feed a baby, she explained how to sterilise it in boiling water before use, and so on. The film crew returned to the village a year later to check her progress and the transformation was remarkable. Not only the film crew, who the year before had been viewed with suspicion, but the welfare worker especially, were welcomed everywhere as friends. She held regular, well attended classes, but the most striking result of her mission of hygiene was that in the past year only one baby had died. This was enlightenment and advancement working through the only way it can: through human common sense. This was harmony in action.

Common sense is usually rated as the lowest of human qualities. 'Use your common sense.' 'His common sense should have told him that.' All such expressions imply that common sense is, or should be, inherent in everyone. This is a remarkably true supposition, for common sense *is* common to every one of us, for the simple reason that it is the voice of reason in every one of us. You could say that it is the lowest gift, the mundane earthly gift; used by the Highest yet accepted by man as nothing more than — common sense! — and if anything, no matter how wrapped up in religious rites or dogma, doesn't 'fit in' with common sense, then it must be rejected.

Referring to Leviticus again, we read in chapter 12 that if a woman has a child, she is automatically unclean. Poor woman! She did what came naturally, but in reparation for the sin of being fruitful, she has to take a year-old lamb to the priest to be offered to the Lord as a burnt offering. She must also take a young pigeon and a turtledove and, after the priest has slit their throats and poured the blood on the altar, her unclean state is miraculously cleansed. Such is the innate piffle we are supposed to believe. (Keep it quiet but men, who set the biological process in motion, get off scot free).

Apart from the apparent stupidity of the ritual, there are two further reasons for rejecting it: the offerings were usually eaten, yet in Genesis it says the command given to man was that 'the fruit of the tree and herbs of the field' shall be food for man, and in Isaiah it says that 'He that killeth an ox is as if he slew a man.' Probably the Bible was passed by the theologians of the time as credible to the public reason, but that doesn't say that their reasoning applies now. The only way to gain from the Bible is to accept that which is logical and to reject that which is stupid and illogical. To reject it completely because of inaccuracies and its long gone superstitions would be as unreasonable as to accept it as being infallible. There is a lot of sound advice and knowledge contained therein, but the wheat must be taken from the chaff and your own common sense will create the division. Blind adherence and the clerical attitude of side-tracking people into false beliefs that a nebulous, wand-waving entity will solve all our problems is holding up progress. This external God, say the Gospels of Matthew and Luke, loves us so much that even the number of the hairs on our head are counted, yet over the centuries thousands of children have died of starvation and it is still happening now in the under-developed countries. Furthermore, there is the tragedy of children being born with afflictions and diseases, and in our times, a whole school of children was suffocated to death by the sliding action of a hill of wet coal slag. In the knowledge of these facts, the counting of hairs sounds a bit fatuous!

Be fruitful and multiply, says the Bible, which is a comforting thought and ideal advice to suit the simpletons who beget far more children than they can provide for or manage. What the Bible excludes is that this advice must be tempered with common sense. In some countries where child deaths are high, parents purposely have a dozen or more children thereby assuring that two or three will survive to provide for them in old age: another instance of the gratification aspect of parenthood. Of course self restraint in the young and vigorous can only be a forlorn hope, especially when the whole material body is geared both by desire and biological impulse for reproduction, but eventually there will have to be a law, enforced by operation if necessary, to restrict the offsprings of adults to say five, otherwise the population increase will lead to more suffering. This is not necessarily an atheistic ideal, but a common sense view based on fact.

In spite of being much maligned, governments, with their laws passed after debate and reasoning, do far more good than all the well-meaning and abstract promises dangled before your nose like a carrot to a donkey which the churches offer as a bait. Governments, by allowing common sense to operate through logical discussion, draw up statutes for the betterment of the people. Laws are passed for the protection of the defenceless, the feeding of the poor, the rights of individuals and recently, in answer to public opinion and pressure, governments now realise that animals may have rights as well. All this is true progress and although debates are not always harmonious, discussion and the application of reason is the only possible way to release mankind from the bondage and superstition of historical stupidity.

Harmony is in all creation, both animate and inanimate. Every cell of the body is part of creation: microcosms within the macrocosm, and every cell, fed on the right sustenance, will conform to the harmony of the universe, free of the discord of disease and sickness.

A lady turned me to vegetarianism. Eventually I advanced further than my tutor and became a fruitarian, for I do believe that if you start anything, it should be pursued to its logical end. Besides, I've worked on farms and seen the cruelty involved in both dairy and meat production. Some say, and I'm inclined to agree, that there is more cruelty in dairy than in meat production, but it is all certainly wrong, being both disastrous to health and degrading to human nature.

The first stirrings towards a reformed diet came when I used to tidy the garden of a vegetarian woman. I became aware that she was 'one of those vegetarians'. She often spoke about her diet and how cruel and unnecessary it was to kill animals for food. For a long time she made no headway, for I continued eating meat and fish as my forefathers had done for generations. To me the lady was a crank. I'd eaten meat all my life and every logical person I had met also ate meat. I used to treat her remarks with the light banter I thought they deserved.

'Ida,' I used to say on leaving, 'I'm going to have a nice juicy steak when I get home.' But she never returned the humour. 'Have you ever thought of the animal killed to give you that meat?' she would reply. However, little do we know of the impact suggestions, apparently neglected by the conscious mind, can have on the subconscious. Her impromptu lessons must have taken root.

I once went into a restaurant and ordered ox heart. Two hearts cut in half were on the plate with the usual two veg. The hearts being cut in half, I could see the ventricles, the aorta and part of the return vein where the blood had been pumped through the animal. Suddenly I felt a revulsion for the meat. I felt like a cannibal about to eat a missionary! I ate the vegetables but left the hearts uneaten — and that was the beginning of my conversion. Later, I tried to overcome my revulsion by eating mince meat when I ate out, but that didn't work. Somehow I knew that flesh-eating was wrong.

Now that my interest was aroused, I started reading vegetarian literature and a whole new avenue of knowledge was revealed. It soon became obvious that the bulk of people, including myself, were completely ignorant about the 'pros and cons' of diet and were governed, not by wisdom, but by habit. For instance, I discovered that Darwin, in his contributions to the study of human origins, clearly showed comparisons existing between anthropoid apes and ourselves both in structure and function, yet all the primates with the exception of man are frugivorous. The apes and all the anthropoids live mainly on fruit, grain and nuts. Dr. F. A. Pouchet in his book *The Universe* goes even further, for he writes, 'It has been truly said that man is fruit eating. All the details of his intestinal canal, and above all, his teeth, prove it in the most decided manner.' Another piece of information I learnt from my reading was that all animal and fish flesh begins decaying immediately the bloodstream is stilled on death of the creature and it is this putrefying flesh, mainly in the large intestine, that is the cause of most illnesses, for the virus is pathogenic.

The casing of the large intestine (colon) is similar to crazy paving, with the capillaries forming the pattern. There is only one cell thickness separating the blood in these capillaries from the food in the colon and feeding is by suction, direct into the bloodstream. The colon is about six feet in length and, on a carnivorous diet, due to the heat of the body, the decaying flesh is in a putrid state by the time it has reached this part of the digestive tract and from this fetid, putrefying mass of food the blood must be nourished. Is it any wonder that the bulk of hospital patients suffer from bowel complaints and diseases in one form or another? With a constipated person the condition is worse. Prior to the large intestine and up to the ileocecal junction which ends the small intestine, the food is broken down by chemical action, so the virus danger is mainly localised in the colon. One writer aptly quotes, 'The sooner we clean up the Augean stables within us, the better it will be for mankind.'

Anna Kingsford, the illumined reformer of Victorian times, wrote,

'The great need of the popular form of Christian religion is precisely a belief in the solidarity of all living things. It is in this that the Buddha surpassed Jesus — in this divine recognition of the universal right to charity. Who can doubt it who visits Rome, the city of the Pontiff, where I now am. I was forced, the day after my arrival, to get out of the carriage in which I was driving to chastise a wicked child torturing a little dog tied by a string to a pillar, kicking it and stamping on it. No one save myself interfered. Today I saw a great, thick-shod peasant kick a mule in the mouth out of pure wantonness. Argue with these ruffians, or with their priests, and they will tell you, "Christians have no duties to the beasts that perish." Their Pope has told them so. So that everywhere in Catholic Christendom the poor, patient, dumb creatures endure every species of torment without a single word being uttered on their behalf by the teachers of religion. It is horrible — damnable, and the true reason for it all is because the beasts are popularly believed to be soulless. I say, paraphrasing a *mot* of Voltaire's, "If it were true that they had no souls, it would be necessary to invent souls for them."

Earth has become a hell for want of this doctrine. Witness vivisection and the Church's toleration of it. Oh, if any living beings have a claim to heaven, surely the animals have the greatest claim of all! Whose sufferings so bitter as theirs, whose wrongs so deep, whose needs of compensation so appalling? As a mystic and occultist, I *know* they are not destroyed by death; but if I could doubt it — solemnly I swear it — I should doubt also the justice of God. How could I tell He would be just to man if so bitterly unjust to the dear animals?'

This was written in 1887. Basically, the attitude of the Church to animals hasn't altered one iota.

It is useless to pull organised religion to pieces and leave a temporal void. Any fool can knock an edifice down but it takes a wise man to build one. Is a plan for a more comprehensive and credible way of life unfolding as the old structure crumbles or are we to be left wandering in a meaningless wilderness? 'People who have rejected religion,' say the clergy, 'wander about in a wilderness of despair looking for an anchor; a meaning to life.' To the institutionalists this may seem to be the case, but it is far from the truth. The grass roots are already well established of a more lasting, logical, and non-harmful way of life, which is springing up from the unfettered mass of lay people: a principle of fidelity and concern for all sentient life; a manifestation of true piety which starts from the lowest, the rejected, the abused, and works upwards from that foundation. A mode of life which is not primarily concerned with self, but with all.

I refer to the many individuals and welfare organisations abroad today. The 'pity they haven't something better to do' elderly spinsters and others who follow the transport of cattle to other lands, exposing the cruelty and abuse involved. These are the true evangelists. The 'interfering' welfare workers who go into the lions' den of evil homes to look after helpless children. These are the true Daniels, the true crusaders. We now have societies for 'Animal Aid', 'Anti Blood Sports', 'Anti Vivisection', 'War on Want', 'Prevention of Cruelty to Children', and countless other humane welfare organisations springing up; but the most sagacious and penetrating of these are the societies connected with the reform of diet, such as the 'Vegetarian', 'Vegan' and the increasing number of fruitarians. For once mankind has been lifted from the degradation of killing in the mistaken belief that it is necessary to kill for food, so will their strength and moral stature grow apace. This is the only sure foundation for advancement by which we will once again regain our rightful place as a rhythmic cell in the harmony of the universe.

And so, as my knowledge increased in this new avenue of awareness, I was moved both by instinct and common sense back to eating the fruit of the tree that man had renounced countless Ages ago. From lacto-vegetarian, I became a vegan, then a raw-food eater, and eventually, on to the ultimate — fruitarian! A book called *The Garden of the Lord* by Hannah Hurnard (now out of print) set me thinking about trying the fruitarian diet again. I had tried it a few years back but got such a hollow feeling that I gave it up. However, my knowledge of what constituted 'fruit' must have been somewhat limited, for the author maintains that the produce of certain vegetable plants such as sweet corn, courgettes, cucumbers, peas, beans, green and red peppers, etc. are also fruits. In a later booklet she advised the intake of grains to supplement the fruit and I have found this good advice. I now take grain in the form of wholemeal bread. Over the year my diet varies a lot, but for some time now I have been having avocado sandwiches for both morning and evening meal, and at midday, fruit with nuts. The sandwiches are wholemeal bread with olive oil and shoyu (a fermented soy sauce) as a spread and this, with sliced avocado between, makes a very satisfying meal; dates, bananas, raisins, or any non-acid fruits can be added if desired.

Midday meal can be: grapefruit, orange, pineapple or any acid fruits with nuts or any other protein. You could swop around and have this for breakfast.

Acid fruits and protein go together; starch and non-acid (alkaline) fruits combine. Really, avocados are high in protein and should not be taken with starch (bread), but I like the taste so much that I throw caution to the wind. I think you can be too faddy on this issue. Sub acid fruits like apples and pears are neutral and I eat quite a lot. I also particularly like grapes, melons, pawpaws, and if I want a special messy treat, indulge in a mango. The diet is strict, but I believe in it for three good reasons. It's the Edenic food stated in Genesis: 'And the herbs of the field and the fruit of the tree shall be food for man.' It's ethically correct, for there is no killing or cruelty involved and also because of the reward: a continual improvement in health.

Some people have the mistaken idea that the diet is expensive, but this is not so, because everything bought is edible and no fuel is needed in either preparation or dish washing. In fact, I find it amazingly cheap. Don't be too fanatical, for adherence to this strict regime lies in resilience and not rigidity. I know at least three local people who were thrilled with the idea of eating only fruit, but gave up after a month or so because they found it 'too restricting'. Therein lies the danger of being too fanatical. The highest of ideals are useless if unworkable. If you want a cooked vegan meal for a change, by all means have one. I often have visitors on Sundays and always give them grapefruit, then a cooked vegan meal and quite enjoy the change myself; but always bear in mind that the more fruit eaten in its natural state, the healthier you are. Muesli or bran and raisins with a plant milk followed by any sweet fruit makes a satisfying breakfast and for midday or evening a 'vegetable' salad makes a change. Cucumber, tomatoes, peas, sweetcorn on a lettuce base with olive oil and seasalt. Grain or any protein can be taken with this. Red, black or white currants go well with any salad. Currants, like grapes, are high in iron and oxygenate the red blood cells: good for anyone anaemic. Grapes are the great antidote to cancer. The two cannot exist together and it is always the grapes that beat the cancer — a veritable case of 'George and the Dragon'. Three of my family died from the disease when they were years younger than I am now, due, in my opinion, to a faulty diet. There are one or two books on the anti-cancer properties of the grape and their contents are irrefutable. One, *The Grape Cure* by Johanna Brandt, is truly remarkable.

Cancer is a putrefactive growth and Johanna Brandt starved the cancer by giving the patient only grape juice on which putrefactive viruses cannot live, for all fruits are fermentative — a totally different organism. Some of her patients, especially the extreme cases, nearly died of starvation but she could tell by the eyes and the colour of the skin when the disease had been conquered; then and only then would she start building them up again on more solid food. The difference in their treatment compared to the medical, is the fact that on the grape cure the body is not only cleared of the disease, but the whole system is purified and rejuvenated during the healing process. Johanna Brandt used the commonsense method.

Recently a programme on the television followed the medical treatment of a young man with cancer. Every ingenious device and drug was used in the treatment by a team of most dedicated doctors and nurses. Computers and a complex network of equipment were in constant use to monitor all the relevant information about the effect of the drugs; heartbeat, blood-counts, etc. After six months he was back at work, but it was obvious that the drastic treatment had worked havoc in his system. Not only did he look twenty years older, but he had lost all his hair and he still had to report back to the hospital for check ups. All concerned deserved the highest praise for their efforts and dedication in saving the man's life and by no means the least deserving was the patient himself for his stoicism, but I still think the best treatment lay in simplicity and not the complexity of science.

But to return to the fruit diet. The choice of fruits is extensive: avocados, apples, apricots, beans, cucumbers, courgettes, coconuts, dates, figs, grapes, grapefruit, lemons, nuts, oranges, peas, peaches, pears, pineapples, raspberries, strawberries, sweetcorn, tomatoes, and other exotic fruits such as pawpaws, kiwi, mangoes. Sprouted grains can be added if you wish. Nuts are mainly eaten for their oil and protein. There is a wide divergence of opinion on how much protein the body needs. Too much, some say, can cause acidity, but I think the amount depends on the nature of your work and activity, plus the fact, that on the fruit diet you get a 'hunch' when you need more, or less, of anything. There is protein in avocados, pulses, bananas, and a small amount in all fruits. However, the main issue to remember is that the life force, the 'Prana' as the Hindus call it, in the uncooked food is as essential to the health of the body as the proteins, calories, and vitamins. However, when considering a fruit diet, some need proof about the different nutrients. So here is a list to satisfy the enquirer:

Energy: (sugar, starch, fat) nuts, bananas, figs, dates, avocados, raisins, seeds. All grains.

Protein: nuts, pulses, avocado, apricots, coconut, bananas.

Vitamins: (A) apricots, bananas, capsicums, melons, strawberries, tomatoes.
(B) nuts, seeds, grains, pulses and other fruits
(C) fresh juicy fruits, blackberries, blackcurrants, oranges, lemons, peppers.
(D) sunshine.
(E) nuts, seeds and grains.

Calcium: sesame seeds, nuts, pulses, figs, currants.

Iron: grapes, dried fruit, nuts, cocoa beans, currants.

Fibres: grains, bran, pulses and all fruit.

To fruit is the ultimate aim of all plants and trees. Fruit is, or contains, the seed of potential life. The rotation is from seed to seed, and by eating fruit we are absorbing life, whereas on a flesh diet, we are taking in death. Consider again the cruelty incurred in the prevalent diet. Animals are butchered by the million to provide food for humans, food which is not only alien to the body, but putrefactive too. The dairy trade is even more atrocious in its exploitation of sentient creatures. Farm animals are denied a natural life. Many bulls spend their lives in semi-darkness, tethered by a short chain from the nostrils to a steel bar. In the ghastly veal trade, calves in dark, cramped pens are fed on skimmed milk, barley and concentrates, then sent to the slaughter house within six months. They have to be, for their kidneys would collapse after that. These and other cruelties are being exposed by animal welfare workers.

With the fruit diet, a few vegetables are permissible. I usually have the savoury vegetable fruits together for a change: peas, cucumber, tomatoes and a protein, but as a rule, raw vegetables are too coarse for humans. When I was a vegan, a lady friend prepared me a colourful dish of grated mixed root vegetables. The plate of food looked very attractive with the different colours ranging out from the centre, but when I got home, I was violently sick. My stomach was obviously passing on the message, 'No thank you!' Fruit and grains, on the other hand, have a finer texture and, being our natural food, never have this effect.

Hannah Hurnard in her book *The Garden of the Lord* maintains that most of the unwholesome food that is eaten is stored in the body in the form of excess fat and in other ways, causing overweight and clogging and the acids in them slowly poison the body, causing distressing and painful diseases. She goes on to say that during the first weeks or months on the fruitarian diet, the first thing the fruit juices do is to break down all the waste matter so that it can be eliminated and this leaves the body purified in a truly remarkable way. However, Hannah made the fatal mistake of being fanatical. From the word 'Go!' it was fruit and fruit only — regardless. Although we must admire her will-power, this rigid attitude can do more harm than good. After three or four years, she had to relax and include grains and vegetables in her menu.

I heard that another writer on the fruit diet gave it up completely and, as I mentioned before, two or three local people I know said they found it too restricting and interfered with their social life. By making a declaration of becoming a fruitarian and then finding, through not using your common-sense, that you cannot keep it up, there is a danger of robbing yourself of the benefits. That is why, in the leaflets I distribute, I advise a cautious approach. The best attitude, in my opinion, is to start by adding more fruit to your usual diet and increase the amount of fruit as the body adjusts to the change. This way is workable, the other way is to court disaster. To use a simile, suppose you got the idea that the jungle natives were right, that by wearing only a loin cloth, the beneficial rays of the sun rejuvenated the body, so you promptly shed all your clothes! The certainty is that the sudden shock of cold to the system would be so great that far from reaping the benefits, you would probably die from pneumonia within a week or so. On the other hand, if you approached it logically and very slowly reduced the amount of clothing you wore, it is much more likely that, as the body adjusted to the new conditions, you would eventually reap the rewards you were looking for. Too sudden and rigid a change can be both physically and psychologically harmful. Accept advice when it sounds logical. For instance, on the fruitarian or vegan diet, doctors maintain that through eating the wrong food over the centuries, the body has lost its capacity to produce the vitamin B12 which is essential to the nerve system and for creating red blood cells, so take the vitamin in some form, just in case! I take it in soya milk (Note: not all brands contain B12. Check the label.) It is a vitamin that the body can store for years, so lack of supply would not be immediately apparent.

I was a lacto-vegetarian for two years, a vegan for fifteen years and at the time of writing, I have been on the fruit diet for five years. Hannah Hurnard, after a similar period, started to include grains into her menu and I have found it essential to eat wholemeal bread, for I seemed to be eating all day and it was only after the inclusion of grain in the form of wholemeal bread that my appetite was curbed and evacuation became more regular. I have read, and it's evidently quite true, that fruit juices liquefy the mucus in the large colon, resulting in too frequent and spasmodic a bowel action, for fruit is a highly concentrated form of vitamin food, but as the bulk of it is liquid, there is a strong tendency to lack roughage. Hannah goes on to say, 'I had seen and understood only half of what God had said in Genesis 1:29. I had not realised that the word translated "seeds" in the English Bible is the usual word for "grains" in the Hebrew Bible — I had completely neglected the grains. Indeed they seem to be God's masterpiece for maintaining health in the physical bodies and for rebuilding everything in them — while the fruits vitalise our mental powers and give wonderful vitality.' Hannah soaked the grains, brought them to the boil, then left them in a heat-retaining box overnight, 'and very sustaining and nourishing they were.' However, wholemeal bread seems to have the same effect in providing the essential nourishment and roughage and is more palatable. Sprouting grains is of course the best method but I always get a slight guilt complex munching away at young life. Bananas used to knock me off colour and too many acid fruits like plums, gooseberries and even oranges gave me twinges of rheumatism, but now they don't bother me; whether this is due to the wheat absorbing the acids or getting acclimatised to the diet, I cannot say.

Nature in organic life is never violent. It builds up, wears away, builds up again and so on. We are, or should be, part of this harmony, a microcosm within a harmonious macrocosm and any ailments during our lifespan are mainly due to three things: environment, pollution and food. Now it is not always possible to overcome the first two obstacles to health, but we can do something about the food we eat. So often we hear or read of 'breakthroughs' in various fields of medicine, but what we should realise is that diseases should not be there in the first place. If we put dirty fuel into an engine the answer to the resultant breakdowns would not be to repair or replace parts, but to make sure that the fuel was clean. This applies equally to the food we consume and although doctors and scientists are full of good intentions their efforts will continue to be in vain until a radical change in diet is advocated for the populace. Eggs, for instance, are recommended as being a good source of protein, yet are used by biologists to propagate putrefactive viruses. George Bernard Shaw had this to say about meat: 'How can people expect good health when they use their stomachs as the graveyard for dead animals?'

Our own body's 'built-in' doctoring technique is much greater than the skill of any specialist. Just give your body the chance to adjust itself to natural foods and the benefits resulting from your own rejuvenating powers will astound you. Ill health is not, as some would have it, a 'karma' that must be worked out, nor is it a trial sent by some nebulous deity, but is a direct result from the ingestion of putrefactive food obtained by killing and cruelty. We must use our common sense and realise that by adopting a non-harming, non-killing, fruit and grain diet, all these so called 'karmas' and 'God-sent trials' will soon melt away. Wearing away through use and age is natural, but imbalance and discord in the body is purely and simply a self-imposed biological process brought about by transgressing natural laws.

And so, perhaps you will see the early childhood impulse that through life spurred me on — on to my present attitude. It has been a seeking where I have always changed as my ideas altered and never hindered the Holy Spirit. As I was led by my common sense and reasoning and knew that what I was doing was right, then I stuck to it through thick and thin. Often on the journey I've looked and felt wretched and been a good advert for doing the opposite to what I was doing, yet slowly and surely the intake of natural food has cleansed not only my body, but my mind and at long last I have emerged onto the tranquil plain of certainty and fulfilment.

From the maelstrom of evil forces in childhood, on to the attainable beauty of life in age.

Ad astra per aspera.

It is the return to Eden!

APPENDIX

THE ABOVE IS THE AUTOBIOGRAPHY of Wilfred Crone which he wrote in the early 1980s.

We know that he submitted it to various publishers but it was not accepted. When asked about it a few months before his death in 1996 (aged 87), he replied 'Oh, nobody wanted it, so I threw it away.'

Shortly after his death, a search was made for any papers or books of special interest. He had tidied up so diligently that none were at first found, but, searching in the airing cupboard, his young friend David Mather found two typescripts of the autobiography. They had each been typed separately and contained variations in one or two parts. The version presented above was prepared and slightly edited by Harry Mather.

Subsequently to the above autobiography, Wilfred Crone wrote some articles for a small circulation magazine/newsletter called *Vegan Views* and these are included in the following pages.

❦

PLANT A SEED

When I was a gardener at the Douglas House Hospital in Bournemouth, I was supplied with all the fruit and greens I needed, for, being on a different diet from the nurses and staff, I fed myself. While I was there, a gang of painters came to redecorate the hospital. I had my meals in my shed and during the 'breaks' one or two often came for a chat. Of course, I didn't miss the chance to spread the word and they all had leaflets about the 'good' and 'bad' things to eat. To put it in a nutshell: fruit and vegetation represented salvation; meat, fish and what-not — perdition! They obviously had more bewilderment than conviction about my 'monkey' diet and used to chivvy me continually. 'I'll bet you've got a rumpsteak hidden somewhere!' was the type of leg-pull I got. 'How on earth did you guess?' I used to parry back, for I always reply to remarks with humour, whether it's light banter or not.

The nurses, by the way, being indoctrinated in medical ignorance, were equally sceptical about it all and used to say, 'If you are ever ill, we'll make your life a misery!' It so happened I was ill once, through lying on concrete in midwinter doing a repair job under a car. Far from the nurses doing what they had threatened, I had enough fruit brought to me to feed a troup of gorillas! But to return to the painters. The foreman was a big, brusque man and although he gave me a hearing, as it were, he was convinced that meat and only meat was the right food on which to work. One evening he told me that his wife had severe rheumatism and could I give her any advice? I gave what advice I could, saying that meat and fish emitted a high content of uric acid in the digestive process and were better avoided in favour of alkaline foods, because the uric acid forms into hard crystals in the joints. He still seemed to have no interest in changing his diet and continued to joke about my hidden rumpsteaks, etc.

However, much to my amazement, the seed must have taken root, for the day they were leaving, he came over to me. 'Wilf,' he said, 'I have something to tell you before I go.' 'What is it, Mac?' I asked, 'Me and my wife and daughter have all decided to change our diet!' I was really surprised because he seemed to be the least likely of all to make such a decision. 'We cannot jump unto your strict diet yet' (at that time I was mainly a raw food vegan) 'but we have decided to go vegetarian first and go on to raw food from there.'

His account of what had happened had an element of humour about it too. 'We had been studying your leaflets,' he went on, 'and when I got home last night, the wife' (I don't know why married men always say 'the wife') said, "If I turn vegetarian, will you?" I agreed because we both think you are right, but when my daughter came in, she went off the deep end. "Dad," she said, "you know my mum isn't in good health and she'll die on that daft diet." We explained that what she was eating now was probably the cause of her rheumatism and that was the reason why we were changing. Anyway, after a lot of explaining and persuading, she suddenly said, "Right! if you are turning vegetarian, I will too!" — So that's the three of us!'

I've found cases like that before, when the least likely have seen the logic in diet reform and done a complete turn about. But, there you are, that's certainly one seed I planted that took root!

All joy to you and yours,

Wilfred Crone

YOU CAN'T WIN 'EM ALL

To me fruit is the answer to all that is wrong with the present conditions, for fruit expresses the omniscience of universal perfection. It is truly 'the food of the gods'. It can unwind the ignorant brain of its frustrations, phobias, and hurts. It heals the body and in the warmth of its released sunlight embraces both sinner and saint alike. By adopting the fruitarian diet one becomes more aware that one is truly part of the universe and by encouraging others along the same path I always hope to bring that awareness in them too.

However, I am prudent in my approach, concentrating first on the vegetarian diet and hoping that, as with me, it will put them on the first rung of the 'Jacob's ladder' leading up to heaven! So please bear with me while I recount some of the reactions I encountered during my quest and accept my apologies if you have heard some before.

While travelling in the car, I used to pick up hitch-hikers and while I had, as it were, a captive audience, I always talked to them about the benefits of food reform. Some seemed interested, others not, but isn't it a pleasant surprise when, by chance, you find that your efforts have borne fruit! Such an instance occurred when I was taking my benefactress (who left me the bungalow in which I now live) to a show garden. I joined the row of cars going into the car park and when I got to the young attendant, I held out the fee. 'No charge, sir,' he said, waving me on. 'How come — no charge?'

I asked. 'You once gave me a lift,' he called as I slowly moved on, 'and I'm a vegetarian now'!

I used to visit Harry Whitfield every Wednesday evening. Harry was a 'born again Christian' and a local preacher. He was also partial to my views but unfortunately his wife and two little girls were unmoved. They believed in reform and redemption — but not of my kind. Harry often said that if the chance came, he would be a vegetarian. One evening when I was leaving, he came out with me to the car. 'Wilf,' he confided, 'the wife and girls are leaving in the morning for a holiday in the Isle of Wight, so I'll go vegetarian while they're away.' 'Is that a promise?' I asked. 'Yes, that's a promise. I'll definitely go vegetarian!' 'You won't regret it,' I assured him as I drove off.

When I visited him the following week, Harry looked a bit embarrassed as he opened the door. 'Have you gone vegetarian?' were my first words. 'Come into the lounge, Wilf, and take a seat while I explain what happened.' I went into the lounge, took a seat and waited. 'Well,' he said, obviously ill at ease, 'I really meant to, Wilf, but the old man in the shop advised me against it.' 'Advised you against it?' I asked incredulously. 'Yes, I went to the health shop last Thursday and told the man serving about my promise to you that I was going vegetarian while the wife was away but, after listening, he advised me against it?' 'What did he say?' I asked in bewilderment. 'Well,' he said, 'you can if you like, but I wouldn't if I were you, because all the vegetarians who come in here look half dead!'

At the hospital where I was the gardener, I often had a chat with the night sister before she went off duty. She was really intrigued by my raw food lifestyle and one morning, to my delight, said she was going to try the vegetarian diet and, hopefully, eventually go on to raw foods. 'I'll start on Monday when I have my two days off,' she assured me. 'Good girl!' I responded. 'You are already on the way to perfect health.'

I caught her in the office on the following Thursday morning. 'How did you get on, sister?' I asked, agog with excitement. 'I went to the health shop on Monday,' she explained, 'but I couldn't get in. In the window were placards with bright yellow stars saying 'this for health' and 'that for health' but a notice on the door said 'Closed owing to ill health'.'

Georgia was a Dutch nurse. She had bought a car but didn't know how to drive it, so asked me whether I would teach her. I didn't need much persuasion! Georgia was a vegetarian and loved nursing old people. She also practised Transcendental Meditation and, although she said it made her calm, I found later that she could get into a flap in the car when surrounded by buses, lorries and impatient drivers tooting their horns. Under stress she also had the habit of using odd Dutch words, which could be disconcerting. 'Am I too near the step? Am I too near the step?' she kept calling above the din of traffic at a busy town crossroads. There were no steps within miles that I could see. 'What's a "step"?' I shouted back above the noise. 'Sorry, I mean pavement,' she called back.

In her driving, I found my pupil had two outstanding points — one good, one bad. The good point was that she would never go above thirty miles an hour. The only trouble was that she went round hairpin bends at the same speed! The bad point was that she hated changing gear, so getting people to scatter out of her way was, to her, the lesser of two evils. It saved the routine of stopping, then going up through the gears again. If you think that old folks in their eighties and nineties can't move fast, you don't know nothin'!

After Georgia passed her test (which was a big surprise to me) the kiss I got was as good as a fortnight's honeymoon and then she asked me if I would continue as her chauffeur because, as she admitted, driving wasn't her forte.

On one outing, a friend of Georgia's came with us. Betty was a vegetarian too — or so we thought. As we were driving along, she was telling us about a good, new café that had opened near the old bus station in Bournemouth. 'Can you get a vegetarian meal there?' asked Georgia. 'Oh, yes,' she assured her, and they have all kind of sandwiches too. I had a chicken sandwich.' 'Just a minute. Just a minute,' I cut in, 'I thought you were a vegetarian!' 'I am,' she answered. 'Well, surely a chicken had to be killed to give you the sandwich?' 'Oh,' was her surprising answer, 'I only ate its body. I didn't eat its spirit!'

The matron was a man and during an interview I asked him whether he would give the patients at least one raw food meal a week. I explained the reasons but he wasn't too enthusiastic. 'We all know about your diet, Mr Crone. I've even put the suggestion to the doctors myself, but they say that geriatric patients need meat protein three times a day, because they don't extract as much nourishment from food as young people do,' he added. I told him that nuts and soya beans were high in protein but, as he said, he had to follow the doctors' orders. which was fair enough.

I seemed to spend more time in the hospital than on the three acres outside. I was always being asked to 'help out'. Anyway on the Friday after the interview, I was indoors and again taking the dinner trolleys to their respective wards. Much to my surprise and joy, I saw that the main course was raw salad with nut rissoles and cheese. The 'afters' were mixed fruits. 'Cheers,' I thought, 'my endeavours have borne fruit,' but there were problems! Two hours later I went back to return the empty trolleys to the kitchen and, passing through a ward, saw a nurse patiently holding a cos lettuce leaf while a toothless old man tried to munch his way through it. 'Hello, Janet,' I called breezily as I passed, delighted to see an old man chewing a lettuce leaf. 'Hello Wilf,' she called back without looking round, then added, 'you and your flippin' raw food diet!'

I used to help myself to any fruit or vegetables that were delivered to the hospital and Bert, a young kitchen hand, assured me that in no way would he adopt my diet. 'Why not?' I asked. The reply was that he wanted to advance in life and not go back to the monkey stage! I could see his point.

Come to think of it, it is rather surprising that I got on so well with the staff and the doctors, for we were viewing health and healing from completely opposing angles. Medical science studies disease to which they say 'flesh is heir' through microscopes and searches for the minute germs that are the cause. The science of natural healing, on the contrary, looks into the infinite for perfect health and not only realises, but proves, that it is the violation of natural laws which is the cause of all ailments and that by the simple process of embracing these laws again, perfect health can be attained. Fruitarians don't look through a microscope — they look through a telescope and see the UNIVERSE. They look into the infinite and see HARMONY and HEALTH!

All joy to all.

Wilfred Crone

& &

KINDLY HERBIVORES

Herbivores are governed in numbers by the food available and the does don't become pregnant while the young are still suckling, which occurs in famine. Genetic weakness only occurs when there is a weakness in one or both of the mating pair; in this case it is magnified in the offspring. Also, the males fight (but not to kill) at mating times, so the strongest carry on the species. In no way is there genetic weakening, nor the necessity of culling by carnivores.

I've worked on dairy farms and only found them dangerous when their life-style was interfered with.

Bulls are only dangerous when kept apart from the herd. Jack Markham, a herdsman, used to sit his children on the bull's back. Once, after milking, we realised a cow was missing. It was now quite dark, so taking a hurricane lamp, I went running up the race that led from the paddock to the yard. Bang! Clatter! Wallop! I went flying up the bull's back between its horns. It had seen me coming and lowered its head. While I picked myself and the lamp up, it showed not the least aggression. Note, these are bulls running with the herd.

Deer are the most nervous creatures of all. I was at a scout camp where a herd of deer roamed free in the wooded private park. When a human appeared, you couldn't see them for dust, stags included.

Hormones activate the body for action, but the type of action is governed by the diet which attunes the brain. Action in the carnivore can lead to killing; in the herbivore it is expended on passive pursuits or strength supremacy.

Mind, I wouldn't be familiar with strange animals, for man has a bad image to them and you must prove yourself the exception before they will react naturally. Don't go charging head on into a strange bull (especially with a hurricane lamp) to prove my point.

Under certain circumstances, such as stress, they will get 'stroppy'. One cow had a still-born calf and when the farmer's wife tried to pick it up, the cow went for her. She managed to escape under a fence, but even then she had two ribs broken and was badly bruised. Luckily it was a poll cow (no horns) or the damage would have been more severe.

Wishing you all joy and goodwill,

Wilfred Crone

THE FRUIT DIET

Providing people are on a reformed diet, then how they interpret it is up to them. I stick to a mainly fruit diet for the simple reason that it suits me. If a vegan diet had suited me, then I still would have been a vegan. I still return to it at times and feel no guilt complex, nor find any detriment to my health. Providing what I consume involves neither killing nor cruelty, then I'm quite happy for I do believe that intake and ethics are related.

Speaking from experience, I wouldn't say that on our reformed diet any precise or involved knowledge is essential, providing a fair amount of our intake is uncooked. In Australia, I have seen herbivore (vegan) animals perfectly fit on the most simple fare. Brombies (wild horses) only eat odd

tufts of grass, yet would gallop through the bush obviously getting rid of surplus energy. Kangaroos could easily keep pace with a car doing 30 mph for long distances, so they certainly were not short of stamina, yet none of these animals had the brain capacity to know that such a thing as a 'science of dietetics' even existed!

On the wider front of economy, politics, etc. the importing of fruit is beneficial to all concerned because it encourages the fruit tree planting and fruit trees are the most prolific source of food production. Also, orchards have, as it were, no time limits. Orchards in Kent and other counties have been producing fruit since medieval times (new trees, of course). On the other hand, there are vast dust bowls in America caused by repeated grain crops.

Few people realise the vast amount of fruit produced by trees in the hotter climes. On a farm in Australia, we had a bower about 10 yards by 20 covered by two Hamburgh grape vines. Not only did we have ample personal supply, but every season a Spaniard collected the surplus grapes in a cart and brewed over 300 bottles of port.

We also had fig trees laden with fruit (the undried Adam fig is the size of a pear). Every morning during the fruiting season, I used to pick a bunch of either 'green' sugar fig or Hamburgh grape as I went to collect the herd at 6 am. I got so full of blood, that often I bled profusely — so anyone anaemic reading this need be anaemic no longer! No one in a country exporting fruit could possibly starve under such Edenic conditions.

Yours sincerely,
Wilfred Crone

PLAYING WITH FIRE!

From earliest known times, humans were acquainted with fire. We know this by charcoal and scorched bones found in caves of the first geological, Palaeolithic period. We must have been pretty ingenious even then, for fire, apart from sun-ray ignition, must be started by friction. Probably this was accomplished by the boy scout method of a stick rotated by a bow or palms of the hand, in cupped wood with light, inflammable material. Fire was evidently used for rendering flesh down to a digestible level; (I suppose dinosaurs were pretty tough!). This places humans, even then, above the modern, most intelligent primates; for apes and monkeys will sit and enjoy the warmth of the fire, but have neither the wit to replenish, nor the intelligence to rekindle the fire when extinct.

And so, from this primeval start, we have pursued the art of cooking and bewitching the appetite until now we are up to the knees in cook books and gourmet recipes, with vegans contributing their fair quota.

Now you can have a body with all the essential nutrients and yet be a corpse if the 'life-force' is missing, so nutrients don't paint the complete picture. In like manner, all food prepared by heat has this essential life-force missing in the cells and is therefore imperfect. Only vegetation can thrive on sustenance drawn from inorganic, lifeless compounds of mineral origin, but all the higher strata of life rely on this basic transmutation. Throughout both the carnivorous and herbivorous worlds, life lives on life and we humans cannot step out of line with impunity. When I was giving out leaflets in Bournemouth, an American visitor told me that in his country there were dieticians who thought that cooked vegan food would keep disease at bay, but not eradicate it.

Then there is the quantity aspect. It takes five minutes to eat an apple, but in less than half that time you could eat three or four cooked ones. A Brussels sprout is the best example of this waste, for it takes ten or more minutes to masticate, whereas half a dozen can be consumed virtually without chewing in much less time. Also, slow mastication is necessary for the saliva to supply enzymes that aid digestion.

Professor Richard Owen FRS maintains that 'The apes and monkeys, which man nearly resembles in his dentition, derive their staple food from fruit, grain, the kernel of nuts ... [which] shows that man was from the beginning adapted to eat the fruit of the trees and the garden.' And to quote Baron Cuvier (notice I mix with all the right people), 'Fruits, roots and the succulent parts of vegetables appear to be the natural food of man. His hands afford him a facility in gathering them and his short and comparatively weak jaws, his short teeth not passing beyond the common line of the others, would not permit him either to feed on herbage nor devour flesh, unless those aliments were previously prepared by the culinary processes.'

Way back in the 18th century, Linnaeus, the observant Swedish naturalist, also advocated the Edenic diet, when he said, 'This species of food (fruit) is that which is most suitable to man: which is evinced by the analogy of wild men, apes, the structure of the mouth, of the stomach and the hands.'

But, Wilfred Crone, the greatest philosopher of all time and known throughout Christendom for his profound pronouncements, sums it all up in the following way, 'Don't be daft — be fruitarian!'

Wishing you all joy and goodwill.

Wilfred Crone

HEALTHY TO THE END

My son, David, and I visited Wilfred Crone regularly during his last years and can confirm that he stayed healthy and active to the end. In his seventies he fractured a hip when the ladder on which he was climbing into the loft fell away from him. He spent some weeks in hospital and some time convalescing with relatives but made a complete recovery.

He would cycle several miles doing his shopping (he was a good customer of the local greengrocer) and did all the housework, house maintenance and gardening himself, taking pains, thought and pride in his work. He had espalier apple and pear trees, also a fig tree and currant bushes. He regularly mowed his lawns, front and back, and kept his hedges well trimmed. He took great pride in the colourful display of flowers in his conservatory.

When he was aged 85, the front wheel of his bicycle jammed and he was thrown violently to the ground on a busy road. He thought that a twig or branch must have jammed the wheel. Fortunately, he broke no bones but was badly bruised. Typically, he was moved by the kindness of the car drivers who stopped to make sure he was all right and offered help. Pluckily, he got back on his bike and cycled home. However, he had badly strained a muscle in his upper leg and could hardly walk when he got home. The pain was often acute, but he struggled on for many weeks using a zimmer frame and for many more weeks he had to use a walking stick. He visited a chiropractor and an osteopath who may have helped the healing process, but it was many months before he was able to regain normal mobility.

Eventually, he resumed his previous level of activity, cycling and gardening as before. He was always on good terms with his neighbours and kept very busy. His house was always kept very clean and tidy and he loved to have visitors, hospitably offering them a well presented fruitarian meal and overjoyed if they expressed their appreciation.

Many young people, who had been sent his leaflets in response to adverts he placed in vegetarian or vegan magazines, such as 'Have a Date with a Peach' and 'Go Bananas', came to visit the man who had inspired them and he loved to feel that his ideas were leaving a legacy.

He remained alert and active both mentally and physically, exploring new ideas. The idea that in advanced age he might have to become dependent on others, instead of being the one providing the hospitality for his guests, was quite abhorrent to him and he often said that people over the age of eighty should be allowed euthanasia.

In his last year he may have been feeling increasingly lonely. A neighbour whom he visited regularly also came from Tyneside and he enjoyed reminiscing about old times and places and her death may have left him feeling more lonely. However, he had no reason to feel lonely in his last week, because a vegan friend had moved to a house close to his and would have visited him, and another had written to ask if he could lodge with him. It seems more as though he had made a firm decision that there was no point in continuing his life. His fruitarian campaign had been taken over by the FRESH Network with a well produced magazine and someone else was distributing his original duplicated sheets, which promulgated the ideas found elsewhere in this book.

He always appeared to be a confident and self-assured person and was so in most ways, but, as he became known to the media, who appreciated his forthright jocular approach (he called himself a 'fruit and nut case'), he was conscious of his lack of formal education compared to that of the interviewers and his humour may have been partly concealing a nervousness that he might fail to put his case to the best advantage and let the side down, for in many ways he was a perfectionist who wanted to achieve the best he could.

When talking with friends he would never admit that he believed in reincarnation, finding the case unproven, but he would usually refer to his experience (which is included in this autobiography) as a tiny child, waking up and saying to himself, 'Eh, I'm back in the world again,' and to his dream of someone whose face was very familiar and whom he felt close to, but whose face he could not identify when he woke up. He was never one to back away from unconventional ideas, so if we do assume that he believed in life after death, I can imagine that he felt he would not make further progress in this life, but could start with a better chance in a future life.

All we do know is that he left a note saying, 'Sorry folks, I don't want to live too long,' and went to find a quick death on a railway line. He must have planned it for days before the event, for he had disposed of many things such as letters and papers, not even dirty linen was left. He may have been preparing for weeks, because he had painted the outside of the house, trimmed the hedges and mowed the lawns. I phoned him on the Thursday evening suggesting I might visit him that night because I was going away on the Sunday, the day David and I usually visited him. He was quick to put me off, saying he had been weeding the garden all day, felt tired and wanted an early night. He said the same to a friend who phoned him every day, but she persuaded him to watch a TV programme she thought he would find interesting. The following day he confirmed that he had watched the programme and insisted he must have an early night that night. Perhaps he had already made up his mind and the early night ploy was meant to prevent anyone contacting him.

On the Thursday, he was seen by neighbours to go out on his bike about 9 o'clock in the evening, which they thought unusual. On Wednesday, he had already left the house keys with a friend across the road without an explanation (the note he left behind told where to find the keys). It was in the small hours of a Saturday in August 1996 that he ended it all.

Why, we shall never know, but we do know that he lived life to the full and he had managed to rise from the 'shadow' of his painful, doubting childhood to the 'sunshine' of conviction and harmony in later years.

For young people to terminate their lives is certainly a cause for regret, because moments of despair eventually pass and lives can be rebuilt and happiness regained. People who have been through terrible ordeals like

Siberian labour camps and Japanese prisoner of war camps have survived to lead useful lives and some even become reconciled with their tormenters. So while there is life there is hope. But there seems little to reproach elderly persons who have already fulfilled themselves and who take their lives with the stated aim of not wanting to be a burden to others.

Wilfred Crone achieved much and came a long way. He had made many friends who sadly miss him. They remain thankful that they had known him, yet feel his loss the more because knowing him had enriched their lives. He often closed his letters saying, 'All Joy and Goodwill,' and that was certainly what those who knew him experienced.

Harry Mather

FURTHER INFORMATION

Readers interested in further information on the dietary ideas and ethical aspects mentioned in this book may contact the following:

THE VEGAN SOCIETY, 7, Battle Road, St Leonards on Sea, East Sussex TN37 7AA, United Kingdom. Send two first class stamps for an information pack. Publishes *The Vegan* magazine quarterly.

VEGAN VIEWS, 6, Hayes Avenue, Bournemouth BH7 7AD. An informal quarterly magazine — a forum for vegan opinion.

THE FRESH NETWORK gives information and guidance to anyone interested in a fruitarian or raw food diet. Send a SAE to The FRESH Network, PO Box 79, Totnes, Devon TQ9 6AX. They also publish a quarterly magazine.

The Information Sheets that Wilfred Crone sent to enquirers can be obtained free of charge from John Rhodes c/o Vegan Views, 6, Hayes Avenue, Bournemouth BH7 7AD.